THE SORROWS OF
YOUNG WERTHER

Johann Wolfgang von Goethe

AUTHORED by W.C. Miller
UPDATED AND REVISED by Jordan Berkow

COVER DESIGN by Table XI Partners LLC
COVER PHOTO by Olivia Verma and © 2005 GradeSaver, LLC

BOOK DESIGN by Table XI Partners LLC

Published by GradeSaver LLC, www.gradesaver.com

First published in the United States of America by GradeSaver LLC. 2006

GRADESAVER, the GradeSaver logo and the phrase "Getting you the grade
since 1999" are registered trademarks of GradeSaver, LLC

ISBN 978–1–60259–052–6

Printed in the United States of America

For other products and additional information please visit
http://www.gradesaver.com

Table of Contents

Table of Contents

Biography of Johann Wolfgang von Goethe (1750–1832)

Goethe (1750–1832) epitomized the Renaissance man in his roles of poet, novelist, scientist, administrator, and critic. He has been referred to as the German Shakespeare, and was a master of the German language. His positions included most of the major posts in the Weimar government, including the Privy Councillor at the Duke of Weimar's court, where he coordinated major mining, road–building, and irrigation projects. In addition, Goethe painted, worked on anatomy and botany, created a theory of colors, and directed a theater for 26 years.

The most complete German edition of Goethe's works, letters, and diaries fills 143 volumes. His novel *The Sorrows of Young Werther*, completed in 1774, is so powerful that it actually inspired many young men and women to commit suicide; the story of the tragic Werther was found on many of their corpses. Goethe's early play *Goetz von Berlichingen*, written in 1773, defined and initiated the storm–and–stress movement of drama (known as Sturm und Drang in German). Two of his later dramas, *Iphigenia in Taurus* (1787) and *Torquato Tasso* (1790), are famous for their classical restraint.

However, Goethe is probably best known for his masterpiece *Faust*, which focuses on the search for the meaning of existence and of the soul. The original publication in 1790 was titled *Faust: A Fragment*. Faust soon became a lifelong obsession for Goethe, who worked on the play for more than 60 years and completed the final draft only months before he died on March 22, 1832. He was 82 at the time. *Faust* elucidated the ideas that no philosophic system can explain the world, that man is not reducible into individual concepts, and that literature can reflect the arbitrariness of life. Goethe's thoughts drew upon and inspired poets and philosophers such as Nietzsche, Beckett and Kafka.

Biography of Johann Wolfgang von Goethe (1750–1832)

About The Sorrows of Young Werther

One of the most famous – and infamous – works in the history of literature, *The Sorrows of Young Werther* was Goethe's first work of narrative art, published in 1774. The novel was perfectly timed, capturing the European imagination with its portrayal of a dangerously sensitive youth driven to suicide. It was an immediate success and launched an entire literary genre, *Sturm und Drang* (Storm and Stress), as well as the career of the modern West's first literary celebrity, Goethe. The novel was a sensation in its time – there was even a Werther perfume for a while, *Eau de Werther* – and has continued to inspire such works as Massanet's opera, *Werther*, Mary Shelly's *Frankenstein* (in which the Monster learns to be human by reading *Werther*), and Ulrich Plenzdorf's 1973 novel, *The New Sufferings of Young W*. It not only helped to create Romanticism, but also provided a vocabulary for adolescent turmoil that has stayed with us to this day. There would be no *Catcher in the Rye* and no *Rebel Without a Cause* without *Werther*.

Famously, the novel is somewhat autobiographical. In 1772, when Goethe was an obscure young legal apprentice living in Wetzlar (in which, presumably, *Werther* is set), he developed an impossible passion for Charlotte Buff, who was engaged to a friend of his, Kestner. The ensuing triangle proved almost impossibly painful for him, and Goethe himself explored the possibility of suicide before moving past his infatuation with Charlotte. Meanwhile, an acquaintance of Goethe's named Jeruselum, while in a similar situation of infatuation with a married woman, shot himself. Jeruselum's story fascinated Goethe, and he married his acquaintance's imagined sufferings to his own experiences, coming up with *Werther*. Goethe treated the writing of the short novel as a cathartic exercise, later writing that he felt refreshed, as though he had just given a "full confession" and was entitled to "new life" upon its completion. However, Goethe's novel was to have an impact disproportionate to its size. What was closure for him opened a wound in Europe's collective consciousness.

Werther's infamy stems directly from the public response to the novel. Not only was the book a bestseller, but it inspired a rash of imitative suicides. Goethe himself, in his later years, spoke of the effect of his book, comparing it to a small spark that exploded a mine full of gunpowder. He writes in his autobiography, *My Life: Poetry and Truth*: "The explosion *Werther* caused was so far–reaching because the young people of that era had already undermined themselves; and the shock was so great because everyone could now burst forth with his own exaggerated demands, unsatisfied passions, and imaginary sufferings." Goethe's era, the late eighteenth century, was primed for his "little book": the energies of youth at that time were bored by a span of relative peace, stifled by the meticulous ideals of neo–classicism, and excited by the new philosophical language of subjectivity and the morbid poetry of English literature. The genre, *Sturm und Drang*, single–mindedly pursues the miseries following from subjectivity, relishing the language of feeling and passion even while it explores the limits of such language, and *Werther* is one of the first and most famous examples of this kind of literature.

Goethe managed to capture the misery and misanthropy of his time in *Werther*, and as a result, life imitated his art. It is a matter of controversy exactly how many youths, dressed in Werther's blue frock coat and yellow waistcoat, were found dead by their own hands with copies of *Werther* in their pockets, but a few undeniably were, and their deaths furthered the stir that the novel had already engendered. Despairing romanticism found its vocabulary in Goethe's first novel, and its legendary mass–suicidal influence made Goethe a celebrity until his death, the first of his kind. Goethe himself came to despise the legions of young men who would pay him a visit only to ask the same questions, "But did Werther really live? Did it all really happen like that? Which town has the right to boast of the lovely Lotte as its citizen?" He writes in his "Second Roman Elegy": "Oh how often have I cursed those foolish pages of mine which made my youthful sufferings public property!"

Werther remains Goethe's most popular work – more popular, even, than *Faust* – though today's readers are likely to view the work with cooler heads than those of the late eighteenth and early nineteenth centuries. The book stands (ironically, for a work obsessed with feeling and spontaneity) as a near–perfectly crafted narrative, carefully observed and expertly executed with many paradoxical details included. Not only is the work a time capsule of sorts, allowing us a glimpse into an age of unrivaled passion and morbidity, but it also transcends its time as a meditation on the extremities of youthful sorrows.

Character List

Adelin

Werther's good–hearted co–worker when he is in his official capacity under the Count.

Albert

Sober, thoughtful, responsible – in a word, the antithesis of Werther – Albert is Lotte's betrothed, and later her husband. At first, he and Werther get along well enough. They are both interesting personalities and incisive conversationalists; indeed, if Lotte had not come between them, they might have been good friends, like Werther and Wilhelm. Instead, Werther's persistent clinging to Lotte drives a rift between Albert and him.

Count C

An aristocratic friend of Werther's while he is working in his official capacity under the envoy. The Count and Werther are kindred spirits of sorts, who are barred from fully realizing their friendship by the social conventions that keep a bourgeois man like Werther from fraternizing too openly with an aristocrat.

Country Lad

A young peasant with whom Werther identifies: he is in love with the widow for whom he works. When his love is foiled, he murders his replacement.

Editor

This mysterious figure steps in to narrate the final part of *Werther*. He is specifically not Wilhelm, nor is he any other known character; he claims to be merely a faithful reporter of facts, but occasionally shows flashes of insight into characters and narrates events from their perspective. His anonymous omniscience seems Biblical.

Envoy

Werther's immediate superior in his position as a court official. The envoy is a meticulous, unhappy man, and impossible to please. Werther despises him, and the envoy dislikes Werther in return.

Fräulein von B

A charming aristocrat whom Werther befriends while working in his court appointment. Fräulein von B. is discouraged from pursuing her friendship with Werther by her snobbish mother.

Frau M

An old woman who lives in a village in the mountains; she requests that Lotte be with her while she dies.

Friederike

Herr Schmidt's sweetheart, of whom he is inordinately jealous.

Hans

Philip's younger brother, a peasant lad of Wahlheim.

Heinrich

A man "in a green frock coat" whom Werther encounters trying to gather flowers in winter. This madman yearns for his happy days in the asylum. It is later revealed that Heinrich was a former employee of Lotte's family, driven insane by his unrequited passion for her.

Herr Audran

Lotte's partner on the night of the dance during which she and Werther meet.

Herr Schmidt

A gloomy fellow whom Werther and Lotte meet during their visit to a village in the mountains.

Lady S, Lady T, Colonel B, Baron F

Aristocratic attendees of a dance thrown by Count C. who are offended by the presence of Werther, a bourgeois, at the party.

Leonora

A young woman with whose sister Werther entertained himself before the novel begins. Werther writes that she was passionately in love with him.

Lotte

Charlotte S., familiarly called Lotte, is forced by her mother's untimely death to act as a mother to her eight younger brothers and sisters – a burden that she accepts cheerfully and selflessly. Writing of the woman on whom the character of Lotte was chiefly based, Goethe said, "Lotte was undemanding in two ways: first, according to her nature, which was intent on creating general good will rather than on attracting any specific attention, and second, she had already chosen someone who was worthy of her, who had declared himself willing of joining his fate to hers for life." In *Werther*, Lotte has pledged herself to Albert, though she feels a special (one might say sisterly) bond with Werther. Werther, for his part, is infatuated with her almost to the point of madness.

Louis

One of Lotte's younger brothers.

Marianne

One of Lotte's sisters.

Minister

The director of the Court for which Werther briefly works. He sympathizes with Werther, though feels that the young man needs to compromise his intensity from time to time.

Old M

Frau M.'s husband, a pleasant enough lower–class man who nevertheless manages his household very stingily.

Philip

One of two peasant boys whom Werther meets in Wahlheim. Werther draws a picture of Philip allowing his younger brother, Hans, to sit in his arms.

Prince ---

A member of royalty whom Werther accompanies and lives with for a short while after resigning from his court position.

S

The bailiff of Wahlheim and the father of Lotte and her siblings.

Selstadt

One of Werther's friends.

Sophy

Lotte's sister and the second–eldest sibling in the family.

V

"An open–hearted youth with pleasant features." Werther converses with this erudite young man, just out of university, in a somewhat condescending way. V. is very enthusiastic about the aesthetic and religious theories he has picked up in school; Werther, however, does not care for such things (though he is careful to show that he knows all about them).

W

A friend of Werther's.

Werther

A young bourgeois dilettante – intelligent but arrogant, artistic but unmotivated – who finds his world topsy–turvy after becoming infatuated with Lotte, a beautiful and good–natured woman who is engaged to the sensible and hard–working Albert. Werther goes through life in his blue frock coat and yellow waistcoat, conversing brilliantly (though rather contentiously) with all who will listen, ruminating on his memories as well as subjective philosophy, and increasingly despairing of life and fate. He has a pensive, outsider's position throughout the work: he loves to observe family life, but is somewhat estranged from his own mother; he wishes to be married to Lotte, but finds himself "just a friend." This estranged sensitivity, exacerbated by his unrequited passion, leads him to commit suicide.

Werther's mother

Werther's mother, who goes unnamed throughout the novel, never directly corresponds with her son. Instead, the two communicate obliquely through Wilhelm. Werther's mother provides financial support for her son, and their estrangement is never fully explained. Werther alludes late in the novel to his hatred for his mother's current place of residence. The unspoken tension between Werther and his mother subtly informs the novel.

Widow

A woman who lives in Wahlheim. Her peasant worker is in love with her.

Wilhelm

Werther's chief correspondent, and the addressee of nearly all of the letters that make up *The Sorrows of Young Werther*. From Werther's interactions with him, we can take Wilhelm to be a sober, sensible fellow – much like Albert – who is nevertheless sensitive to Werther's own more tumultuous character and a true friend. In order to get over his feelings for Lotte, Wilhelm encourages Werther to take a position in a legal capacity for a Count, advice that Werther follows only to resign in a huff and return to his impossible infatuation.

Woman of Wahlheim

The daughter of the schoolmaster, and the mother of Hans and Philip. Werther rests under her linden tree. Her husband is in Switzerland, trying to collect his inheritance from a cousin. Near the end of *Werther*, Werther learns that this family has met a tragic fate.

Pastor of St. ---

The pastor of a small village that Werther visits with Lotte. Werther looks back on his time with the pastor nostalgically.

Wife of the New Pastor of St. ---

"A foolish woman who pretends to erudition." She cuts down the walnut trees on her property and argues theology all day, cultivating the ire of the commoners of her village as well as that of Werther.

Major Themes

Class

Why is Werther so unhappy in his official position? One could easily cite several reasons. First of all, his temperament is not suited to sitting around in an office all day; second, he is incapable of the meticulous attention to boring details that marks the life of a Court official. But underneath these personality–driven conflicts lies the question of class: Werther cannot stand being snubbed.

In fact, Werther's snubbing in Book Two – which drives him back to Wahlheim and suicide – is only the most obvious manifestation of class assumptions in the novel. During Book One, Werther speaks of his relationship to the peasant class around Wahlheim quite fondly. In fact, Werther sees the simple drama of the peasants in their naive "patriarchal" society as beautifully poetic; his entire theory of art privileges a simplicity of expression that only the lower classes seem capable of. Werther could not hold this opinion if he were not of a higher class than they. He speaks from a position of privilege, and though his attitude toward the peasants is kind, it is also patronizing. There is no doubt that he feels himself superior; their naive charm is only virtuous because he – the idle youth with nothing at hand but time and his mother's money – says it is.

The beginning of Book Two provides a startling contrast to Werther's seeming life of privilege: Werther, it appears, may have been able to stay away from Lotte after all had been accepted by high society. Instead, he finds himself amidst the injustices of the class system, humiliated by people whom he believes he is smarter and more talented than. Werther's position is tricky; as he writes, he realizes the advantages he himself has reaped from the class system, but when he is on the bottom of the social ladder these advantages don't amount to much. His behavior at Count C's party confirms Werther's discomfort with either conforming to class conventions or outwardly rejecting them: he remains at the party even though he is unwelcome, and when he is unsurprisingly snubbed, he throws a tantrum and leaves. Perhaps if he had been able to rail against the follies of the upper class as a member of privilege himself (just as he criticizes the bourgeois class from within elsewhere in the novel) he would not have fled to Wahlheim, where there were no nobles to irk him. In this light, being born bourgeois instead of noble may be Werther's greatest sorrow of all.

Family

Werther has mother trouble – there can be no doubt about it. He never directly insults his mother, but his dislike for her is sprinkled throughout the narrative. For example, he never contacts her directly, instead relying on Wilhelm. Further evidence is found in the bitter tone of the letter of May 5, 1772, when Werther mentions his mother's decision to leave the place of his birth. One of the major focal points in *Werther* is Werther's need to compensate for a strained home relationship. He needs a family – if not his own, than another's. In search of this idealized family, he stumbles across Lotte's. Her family is relatively serene, even given the early death of her mother and the abundance of mouths to feed. It has the two things that seem to matter to Werther most in a family: lots of children, and an intensely loving mother figure.

Werther's view of childhood appears to be ambiguous. On the one hand, in his letter of May 22, 1771, Werther sees children as the height of vanity, living happily because they are ignorant, fearing no principle but the rod and delighting in no principle but candy and toys. This cynicism is absent, however, after Werther meets Lotte and her eight brothers and sisters. His letter of June 29, 1771 is virtually an encomium to children. He alludes to Jesus Christ's order to his followers to emulate children, and writes, "Any yet, dearest friend, we treat them, who are our equals, whom we should look upon as our models, as our subjects." Werther finds complexity in the simplicity of childhood; there is no doubt that he is happier on the whole in the company of children then he is moving amongst adults.

Just as complex is Werther's attitude toward motherhood. Goethe's works often praise the feminine in ways that may make modern feminists uncomfortable. Goethe's last words in *Faust, Part II*, which translate, "The Eternal Feminine draws us upward," express this position. Goethe seemed to feel that modest, cheerful wifehood and motherhood were paragon states to which every man ought to strive, but which no man can really attain. Werther expresses this opinion even before meeting Lotte (who is, obviously, the perfect woman: motherly and virginal) when he writes of Hans and Philip's mother, "The tumult of my emotions is soothed by the sight of such a woman, who is rounding the narrow circle of her existence with serene cheerfulness, managing to make both ends meet from one day to the next, seeing the leaves fall without any thought save that winter is near." Like his attitude toward the lower classes, this is at once beautiful and condescending.

Goethe, however, does not simply endorse Werther's opinion. After all, Werther does not attain this idealized family life – he merely writes about it. Lotte herself alludes to Werther's tendency to idealize people when she says, near the novel's end, that Werther pursues her only because she is impossible to attain. Lotte is more than a good mother/sister – she is a smart, thoughtful woman who holds true to her principles. In the end, Werther's obsession with Lotte's motherliness reveals more about his own impoverished upbringing than it does about Lotte herself.

Happiness

Werther has a lot to say about happiness, and, in typical fashion, his feelings on the matter are often inconsistent. The one consistency: whenever he says he has attained happiness, despair is just around the corner. He writes in his letter of August 18, 1771, "Must it so be that whatever makes man happy must later become the source of his misery?"

For Werther, it seems, the answer is "yes". He is happy with Lotte, but suicidal because he cannot have her; he is happy with Fraeulein von B, but it is his attachment to her that positions him to be insulted at Count C's party. Every instance of happiness becomes an opportunity for Werther to be made unhappy. Furthermore, Werther seems painfully aware that it seems to be his destiny to spread his unhappiness and discord among his friends. Even poor Wilhelm, with whom Werther is on such good terms, is made to suffer simply because Werther must tell his someone of his misery.

It is more than a little ironic, then, that Werther is so contemptuous of "bad moods." He writes of Albert, "He seems seldom to be in bad moods, a sin which, as you know, I hate more in human beings than any other," and one of his major reasons for loving Lotte so much is her constant cheerfulness. Werther feels that the worst thing one can do is to ruin someone else's happiness with gloom and doom, as Herr Schmidt does in the letter of July 1, 1771. But Herr Schmidt is just mildly crabby; Werther, with his full–blown suicidal depression, manages to ruin others' happiness on a scale that Herr Schmidt would never be able to manage. Werther's attacks on bad moods – like his occasional blanket dismissals of the possibility of sustained happiness – appear to be inwardly directed: he attacks in others the things he hates in himself.

The Limits of Language

For someone who spends so much time writing letters, Werther does not have much faith in language. When trying to explain the country lad's love for the widow in his letter of May 30, 1771, he pauses, writing, "No, words fail to convey the tenderness of his whole being; everything I could attempt to say would only be clumsy." This distrust is not just theoretical: he puts it into practice, too, especially late in the book, when he writes, "It makes me angry that Albert does not seem delighted as he – hoped – as I – thought to be, if – I am not fond of dashes, but it is the only way of expressing myself here – and I think I make myself sufficiently clear."

In the two above examples, Werther's turbulent spirit is expressed in two ways – first, he refuses to relate a peasant's story in conventional phrases, and second, he attests to the lack of clarity in his own feelings when he declares the dash–riddled sentence above "sufficiently clear." In the first case, he emphasizes the cheapening effect of language. Werther fears employing the trite, conventional, quotidian phrases that everybody else uses; he wants language that is true to his unique, extremely sensitive way of seeing the world. Such language, as we see in the second case, is hardly coherent, because *he* is hardly coherent.

This complicated issue – the use of language to destroy the boundaries of language – is also the essence of Romanticism. Werther (and Goethe) reveal to readers the limits of the polished, precise diction of the Enlightenment. Alexander Pope's neat heroic couplets are not suited to Werther's turmoil, because Werther's turmoil is not neat. By appealing to the new, extremely subjective, anti-language of feeling, Goethe loses the precision of rational grammar and punctuation, but gains the power to express the irrational.

Stormy Weather

Werther and the weather – the two words are quite similar and so, in fact, are their dispositions. Constantly in flux, elemental, unpredictable...and when the weather is stormy, Werther's temper is often stormy, as well. Sometimes his mood is stormy in a "good" way – such as when he experiences nervous joy during the dance with Lotte – but it is more often stormy in a "bad" way. As the weather worsens, Werther's suicidal tendencies become even more apparent.

In *Werther*, the outside world frequently mirrors or compliments the inside world. Indeed, the very word "nature" is a kind of pun, referring both to the natural world around us and to the truths at the depths of our being. In *Werther*, the distinction between these two realms of nature is blurred: each, it seems, influences the other.

As in later works of Romanticism, such as Turner's landscapes or Shelly's nature poetry ("Mount Blanc", for example), Goethe finds great power in the contemplation of untamed natural forces – so different from the neatly trimmed gardens of the Enlightenment. The genre he started with this book wasn't called *Sturm und Drang* for nothing. And the storms – always – are as much an expression of the power of human feeling as the power of the natural elements.

Subjectivity

It is difficult to select a catch–all term for the kind of literature *Werther* helped to initiate. There are plenty of options: one could call it Romantic, *Sturm und Drang*, or the Literature of Sensibility, just to name a few. But one concept that seems to be at the heart of Goethe's youthful novel, and the later genres that were so inspired by it, is subjectivity. Werther fascinates himself; he studies himself; he knows himself. He tirelessly thinks about – and writes about – his language use, his perceptive faculties, and his thoughts. In fact, he writes about almost nothing else. Any letter in *Werther* is focused on the search for the self.

Today, with abundant confessional poetry, post–modern art and tabloid magazines, self–reflection is everywhere. In 1774, however, this wasn't the case, and the freedom to study oneself, one's feelings, was a new and liberating thrill. To be misunderstood by the population in general, and to find true comfort only with other initiates of the secrets of subjectivity (readers of Klopstock, Ossian and Goethe) was to be a rebel. The late eighteenth and early nineteenth centuries were incredibly exciting, turbulent years, during which our modern emotional vocabulary was more or less forged from scratch in response to the complacent philosophies of the Enlightenment. Certainty was becoming less and less certain;

Major Themes

objective appraisals of the world and its inhabitants were growing more and more complicated. The human being was beginning to be defined not by order, but by contradictions.

Werther is the quintessential early romantic. He is extravagantly self–absorbed, hopelessly restless, always out–of–breath about some less–than–rational opinion, and proud of his contradictions, proud of his suffering. He spends much of his time contemplating the way in which his self–knowledge is complicated – the way in which he still does what he knows will make himself and others unhappy. This is because it does not matter what he *knows* about himself: he will always give way to what he *feels*.

Suicide

Suicide is Werther's constant companion far before the actual moment of his death. As early as the letter of May 22, 1771 Werther mentions it, often ending his gloomier letters with a hint at his suicidal tendencies. In fact, Werther never really thinks of death without thinking of his own death.

Suicide is, in *Werther*, the threshold of the self, and the self is everything. It is the clearest expression of man's own self–sufficiency. He writes that a man, "however confined he may be...still holds forever in his heart the sweet feeling of freedom, and knows that he can leave this prison whenever he likes." Is there any doubt that Werther will commit suicide, sooner or later, in one way or another? He seems destined to do so, and comfortable with that destiny. After all, Werther argues with Albert about how "natural" suicide is: someone who sees life as a sickness can cure his misery with a simple tug on a trigger.

Despite the protagonist's uncomplicated willingness to embrace the act of suicide, Werther's own suicide is one of the most ambiguous events in the novel. This is not because of Werther, but because of Albert and Lotte. In a novel where almost everything is answered and explored at length, one of the great mysteries of *Werther* is whether or not Lotte and Albert approve of Werther's act. He asks them for the pistols, and they give them to him, fully aware of his fixation on suicide. Werther himself takes this as a sign of Lotte's approval, and is somewhat cheered. After the deed is done, however, the editor writes, "I cannot describe Albert's consternation, Lotte's distress."

In Albert and Lotte's turbulent, tortured attitude toward Werther just before and after he pulls the trigger lies the suggestion that suicide is not as simple and natural an act as Werther makes it out to be. His shuddering, still alive near–corpse, his death rattle – these horrible images deflate the romanticism of suicide in the final moments of the novel. However, the eighteenth century Werther enthusiasts who followed in their hero's footsteps did not heed these warnings. Indeed, in modern psychological parlance, copy–cat suicides are said to be caused by "The Werther Effect." This is a book that makes the case both for and against suicide. Werther makes the case for it; Goethe – in his careful cultivation of Werther's shortcomings and final emphasis on the brutality of the act – makes the case against it.

Glossary of Terms

anglaise

An English country dance. Famous pieces composed according to this dance form are Bach's *English Suites*.

Batteux

Charles Batteux (1713–1780) was a leading Catholic philosopher of the eighteenth century. He wrote famously on aesthetics, arguing that one can evaluate poetry according to the taste and precision of its expression. Werther, one can assume, finds Batteux a pedantic bore.

cabriolet

A small two–wheeled carriage with a folding top.

clavichord

A precursor to the piano, the clavichord is a small keyboard instrument in which metal strings are struck with metal blades known as tangents. The sound of this instrument is soft and delicate, somewhat like a toy piano. Almost all baroque and classical keyboard music can be played on a clavichord, and much of this music was composed on one.

Colma

Salgar's bereaved lover in Ossian. He has killed Salgar's brother in battle.

contredanse

Any French dance based on English folk dances where ladies and gentlemen face each other in two lines. Contredanse can also mean a piece of music meant to be danced to in this fashion.

de Piles

Roger de Piles (1636–1709) was the pseudonym of Francois Tortebat. He was a French art critic of the seventeenth century.

duodecimo

A small book, about the size of a trade paperback.

Emilia Galotti

One of Lessing's best–known plays, which first appeared in 1772. The title character is a beautiful middle class woman whose chastity is under siege by a nobleman; she has her father kill her rather than endure disgrace. This tale of bourgeoisie tragedy (and assisted suicide, in Galotti's case) has some parallels with Werther's. One of the models for Werther, Goethe's young acquaintance Jeruselum, committed suicide with *Emilia Galotti* open on his writing desk.

en passant

French for "in passing."

Ernesti

Johann August Ernesti (1707–1781) was a Dutch theologian, philologist and editor of Greek classics. Werther is alluding to his edition of Homer, published 1759–1764.

Fingal

Ossian's father in Gaelic myth.

Francis I

(1708–1765). The Holy Roman Emperor and the Grand Duke of Tuscany.

Heyne

Christian Gottlob Heyne (1729–1812) was a German classicist and archaeologist. Werther has no interest in his learned approach to the sublime.

Hofrat

An official German administrative position. Ironically, perhaps, given Werther's distaste for titles and trappings, Goethe himself is the most famous man ever to have held this position.

Homer

The legendary ancient Greek poet to whom the Iliad and Odyssey are ascribed. During the first half of *Werther*, Homer is Werther's favorite (one might say only) poet.

in qualitate

Latin. Literally, "in quality," meaning in this context, "among people of quality."

Karlsbad

A German resort with natural springs.

Kennicot

Benjamin Kennicott (misspelled in the text) (1718–1783) was an English theologian and Hebrew scholar.

Klopstock

Friedrich Gottlieb Klopstock (1724–1803) was a German poet with a religious temperament. Klopstock anticipated and inspired the Romantic sensibility. The "ode" alluded to is "Wingolf" (1767), a rewriting of Klopstock's 1747 ode, "To My Friend". Lotte's allusion to this ode suggests that she sees her connection with Werther as one of exalted friendship.

Lavater

Johann Kaspar Lavater (1741–1801) was a German poet. He composed odes and epics in the style of Klopstock. Following the publication of *Werther*, Lavater and Goethe became good friends, though Goethe later broke off their friendship, accusing Lavater of vanity and superstition. Lavater is chiefly known today for his work in physiognomy, the science of distinguishing faces.

Lessing

Gotthold Ephraim Lessing (1729–1781) was a renowned German playwright and theorist. He was the first German playwright to champion the bourgeoisie as a worthy subject of literature.

Levite

A descendant of the tribe of Levi. Werther seems to use this term to refer to the Pharisees, a sect of Judaism much maligned in the gospels. They are known for their pride and self–righteousness (see Matthew 9:11, Luke 7:39, 18:11,12).

linden trees

Large, shady deciduous trees. Linden trees have a special place in German folklore – and thus in the Romantic imagination. They are associated with melancholy, death and mystery.

Michaelis

Johann David Michaelis (1717–1791) was a German biblical scholar.

Miss Jenny

Werther's catch–all term for an average young woman.

nosegay

A bouquet

Ossian

A legendary Gaelic poet, son of Fingal. James MacPherson, a Scottish poet, published many poems of Ossian claiming to have translated them from ancient Gaelic; it later turned out that he had composed them himself. Goethe treats

Ossian as though the MacPherson controversy does not exist.

paladin

A champion knight.

Penelope

In the *Odyssey*, Penelope is Odysseus' faithful wife. She resists the pressure of countless suitors to remarry while her husband is lost at sea; meanwhile, these suitors slaughter the beasts of her household and stage an endless feast at her expense.

pro forma

A Latin phrase meaning "as a matter of form."

raree show

A peep show played by mechanized figures in a small, often coin–operated theater.

Salgar

In Goethe's translation of Ossian, the deceased lover of Colma.

Selma

A mythical figure who, in Ossian, holds a feast where bards contest.

Semler

Johann Salomo Semler (1725–1791) was a seminal German biblical commentator and church historian.

Sulzer's "Theory"

Johann Georg Sulzer (1720–1779) was an Enlightenment philosopher of Mathematics. His "theory" refers to his work on electricity. (It is apropos for Werther, so concerned with the storms of nature, to belittle an Enlightenment theorist's attempts to explain the science behind storms.)

The Vicar of Wakefield

A novel by the Irish author, Oliver Goldsmith (1730–1774). Goldsmith was one of Goethe's (as well as Werther's and Lotte's) favorite authors. The novel depicts the trials and tribulations of a provincial vicar, celebrating above all the joys of family.

Ullin, Ryno, Alpin, Minona

The "bards of song" in Ossian.

Wetstein

R &J Wetstein was an eighteenth–century publishing house.

Winckelmann

Johann Joachim Winckelmann (1717–1768) was a German archaeologist. He admired the harmony and quiet grandeur of Greek and Roman sculpture.

Wood

John Wood, the Elder (1704–1754) was an English architect. His son, John Wood, the Younger, was also a famous architect. Many of Wood's buildings feature the symbolism of Freemasonry, a famous brotherhood that espouses Enlightenment ideals.

Glossary of Terms

Short Summary

The Sorrows of Young Werther, a novel that consists almost entirely of letters written by Werther to his friend Wilhelm, begins with the title character in a jubilant mood after having just escaped from a sticky romantic situation with a woman named Leonora. Werther has settled in a rural town, determined to spend some time painting, sketching, and taking excursions around the countryside. Werther does not accomplish much work, preferring to admire the easy lifestyle of the peasant class, which reminds him of the ancient "patriarchal life" found in the Bible. Werther makes the acquaintance of many of the local peasants, including two peasant brothers, Hans and Philip, and a country lad who is in love with the widow who employs him.

Werther finds Wahlheim, a village a short distance away from his town, to be the most charming place in the countryside. This estimation increases a hundredfold when he meets the village bailiff's daughter, Lotte, at a dance. Their interaction is immediately striking – they are both enthusiasts of the new sentimental style of literature, represented by Goldsmith and Klopstock, as well as ancient writers like Homer and Ossian. Lotte, however, is engaged to an upstanding man, Albert. Werther must satisfy himself with friendship alone.

In the coming weeks, Werther grows more and more impressed with Lotte, cherishing her unique charm and insight as she uncomplainingly carries the burden of motherhood. She is the eldest of eight children, and assumed the responsibility of caring for her siblings after her mother's death. However, Albert returns, and Werther must meet the man who has Lotte's heart. After determining that he will leave, Werther instead stays, forming a friendship with Albert, who he finds to be both intelligent and open–minded, though much more sensible than the romantic Werther.

Upon Albert's arrival, however, Werther grows increasingly infatuated with Lotte. He can't resist feeling that Lotte would be happier with him; they are both initiates in the intense, subjective emotionalism of *Sturm und Drang*, and Albert is not. However, the faithful Lotte has no intention of leaving her fiancé, and Werther determines, at Wilhelm's recommendation, to take an official court position rather than remain in an impossible triangle. He leaves Wahlheim without informing Albert or Lotte of his plan.

Werther's official position, however, is a great disappointment to him. He clashes with his employer, the envoy, who is as meticulous and cerebral as Werther is spontaneous and emotional. Werther also loathes the social scene of his new job, in which the aristocratic class rules over all, though he cultivates rewarding friendships with two aristocrats, Count C and Fräulein von B. The positive aspect of his job crumbles, however, when the aristocratic class, including Fräulein von B, snubs Werther at one of Count C's parties. Humiliated, Werther resigns from his position, moving with another friend, Prince –––, to the Prince's country estates. This situation, too, is short–lived, as Werther finds himself irrevocably drawn back to Wahlheim and Lotte.

When Werther returns to Wahlheim, he discovers that his infatuation with Lotte has only grown stronger during the separation. As Lotte later suggests, it seems that the impossibility of his possessing her is what feeds his obsession. Albert and Werther become increasingly estranged, and Lotte is caught in the middle. Also, the countryside has taken a turn away from the idyllic: Hans is dead, and the country lad's tale of love has ended in murder. Meanwhile, Werther meets Heinrich, a former employee of Lotte's father's, who was driven mad by an unrequited passion for her. Werther feels increasingly hopeless.

Three days before Christmas of 1772, in an attempt to salvage what is left of their relationship, Lotte orders Werther not to visit her until Christmas Eve, when he will be just another friend. Werther decides that he cannot live on such terms with Lotte, electing instead to kill himself. He pays Lotte a final visit, during which he forces a kiss and is ordered never to see her again.

At home, alone, Werther writes Lotte a letter. He asks her for Albert's hunting pistols, and she sends them to him. Then, with a calmness hitherto unknown to his restless soul, Werther shoots himself in the head. He lingers until the morning; Lotte, Albert and Lotte's brothers and sisters watch him die. At the novel's end, Werther is buried without a church service. Lotte's own life is in jeopardy as well; she is driven to desperate grief by Werther's action.

Summary and Analysis of Book One: Letters of May 4–May 30

Summary

After a very short note from the editor encouraging the reader to sympathize with Werther's tragic fate, *The Sorrows of Young Werther* begins with Werther in an ebullient mood, having escaped a young woman named Leonora, whom he implies was madly in love with him. Werther has retreated to a quiet country setting in Germany with the intention of spending his time drawing. He has left behind both his best friend, Wilhelm, and his mother, who is left unnamed. Werther and his mother do not seem to get along particularly well – a fact that we can assume because he never addresses her directly, instead speaking to her through Wilhelm. He notes, however, that he has taken care of some family business stemming from a disagreement between his mother and his aunt.

Werther is not a very diligent artist; he spends most of his time wandering the nearby rural regions and observing the customs of the peasant class. He finds the peasants enchanting and watches them as they go about their daily tasks. When he sees young women fetching water from a local well, Werther is reminded of the women in the Bible who do the same. In general, he sees the countryside as operating according to an ancient patriarchal code, untainted by the influence of erudition.

Several more examples reveal how Werther has had enough of book–learning. He tells Wilhelm not to send his library, saying that he is happy to read his Bible and his Homer – nothing more. Later, Werther dryly relates a conversation with a young man he calls V., who is enthusiastic about the latest Enlightenment thinkers and theories. Werther likes V. but is rather condescending toward his learnedness. Another acquaintance Werther makes is the Prince's bailiff, S. He notes that the bailiff's eldest daughter is much admired—Werther, too, will come to admire her, to say the least.

Although he takes joy in his surroundings, Werther's gloomy side is apparent right from the start. He writes that he finds many of the people he meets "thoroughly repulsive and quite intolerable in their demonstrations of friendship." He also states that the happiest people are the most ignorant – those who lack the intelligence or the curiosity to see the injustice of the world. This haughty note is complemented by an obsession with death. In the letter of May 22, Werther alludes to suicide, saying that through it one can "leave this prison whenever he likes."

Werther writes that he has taken to wandering over to a charming nearby village, Wahlheim. While there, he makes the acquaintance of the local landlady and some of the peasant children. He makes a sketch of two peasant brothers that depicts the elder allowing the younger to rest in his arms. Werther thinks his sketch is marvelous (not a modest man, he...) and attributes its success to the spontaneous beauty of nature. He also meets the brothers' mother, whose husband has gone to Switzerland to retrieve his inheritance from an obstinate cousin.

Also in Wahlheim, Werther meets a young "country lad" who has a rather tragic story to tell: he is in love with the widow he works for and pines all day long for her. Werther finds the rustic eloquence of the country lad as he talks about his beloved just as beautiful as the most perfectly crafted poems of the intelligentsia. He admires spontaneous passion that is imperfectly expressed and channeled through raw nature.

Analysis

First, a word about the editor's note with which the novel opens. Elizabeth Mayer and Louise Bogan's otherwise very good translation of *Werther* leaves out this opening note, to the detriment of the work. The note is important because it serves as a framework for the novel. First of all, it spoils the "surprise" of the ending, as it suggests that Werther meets an untimely fate. This is important to a full reading of the novel, however, as the reader should have no illusions that Werther's tale might end happily. Second, the epigraph exhorts those who might follow Werther's example to take solace in their pain by reading about Werther's. Goethe presents his book as a friend and companion – essentially the equivalent of a living pen pal like Wilhelm. Of course, historically, *Werther* probably incited more suicides than it prevented, but Goethe included the note specifically to warn readers against this possibility. Finally, the epigraph emphasizes the fact that this volume is edited. This is Goethe's ambiguous gesture toward verisimilitude—he pretends that an "editor," either he or someone else, has collected all of the available documents about Werther's tragic end. It is important to keep in mind while reading *Werther* that Goethe wants us to know that the story is edited and organized from a perspective other than Werther's. In the original 1764 edition of *Werther* this editorial hand was quite subdued, but he especially emphasizes the role of the editor in the revised edition of 1787, the version that is almost always read today. At the close of the novel, the editorial perspective will become especially important.

Just as the editor's note contains the seed of tragedy that will grow over the course of the novel, so the first six weeks of letters provide us with a fairly complete portrait of Werther, emphasizing his shortsightedness as well as his likeability. Werther does not, in truth, change a great deal over the course of the novel; his tragic potential and suicidal personality merely unfold according to their own logic. Goethe is the master of the *Bildungsroman* (which roughly translates "Novel of Education"), a novel form in which the kernel of nature in a protagonist comes into its own through narrative action. Even in this, his first work of fiction, Goethe operates according to the rule of the *Bildungsroman*. Werther does not do anything unlike him; the possibility of his suicide is present from the first words of the book, in the editor's note. Lotte's rejection merely catalyzes his natural chemistry.

However, in the first letters that he writes to Wilhelm, Werther is nearly always happy. He observes the world with acute sensitivity, always aware that all observations must come from himself. Indeed, Werther's own subjectivity fascinates him. (This is the same era, it is worth mentioning, during which the European stage was set for the subjective philosophy of Kant and his followers.) For example, in his letter of May 10, Werther writes, "I am so happy, dear friend, so completely sunk in the sensation of sheer being, that my art suffers. I could not draw anything just now, not a line, and yet I have never been a greater painter than at the present moment." What, one might ask, does Werther mean by that? Werther uses this paradox to illustrate his reflective state. For Werther—and for Romantics in general, of all eras and ages—perception of nature itself is a kind of painting. Because we always play an active role in interpreting the world—through our eyes, ears, noses, tongues, and flesh—we are, in a way, *painting* the world. This deep inner communion with outer and inner nature, in all its confusion, is the most emblematic attribute of the *Sturm und Drang* (Storm and Stress) movement in Germanic literature, of which *Werther* is the preeminent example.

Werther's intense subjectivity provides a basis for his theory of art, which he outlines extensively in his letters of May 26 and May 30. The dominant aesthetic theory at the time of *Werther*'s publication held that beauty was revealed through rules—that it is through form and constraint that art comes to be. Werther admits that there is some truth in this opinion, but contends that truly overwhelming beauty follows from nature itself. In the simple–yet–profound, unstaged charity of one peasant brother caring for another, for example, Werther sees a glimpse of the infinite, the sublime. He is so passionate in his feeling that truth and beauty reveal themselves best in unadorned nature that he mocks anyone who attempts to learn about these absolutes through schoolbooks or theories (such as poor V.). The Enlightenment, he thinks, has got it all wrong. The true locus of beauty is not in the intellect or in reason, but in natural feeling and passion. It is worth adding that Goethe himself, though certainly sympathetic to Werther's passion, does not see things so simply; his novel, in fact, is a work of form, "rules," and intellect just as much as it is a passionate, unadorned outpouring of the heart.

Werther is undeniably a very interesting fellow: he rejects the erudition and rationality popular during his age, and has lovely, poetic things to say about himself. However, one cannot overlook his many obvious flaws. Remember, for example, that the novel is composed almost entirely of letters to Wilhelm. How often does he ask about Wilhelm, or about his mother? How much genuine interest does he show in anyone except himself? Even when he praises others, Werther is primarily praising his own perception of that person. Werther's standard for judging whether someone is worth his time is quite simple: he asks himself, "How brilliant does this person think I am?"

Also, Werther has a complicated relationship with the lower classes. He is a youth of obvious privilege. Though he is estranged from his mother, he is financially dependant on her, and spends his days doing essentially nothing—pretending to draw. Of course the laborers fascinate him: he hasn't done a day's work in his life. Furthermore, his idealization of lower class workers actually disguises a strain of snobbery. He writes of the peasants, "I know quite well that we are not and cannot ever be equal; but I am convinced that anyone who thinks it is necessary to keep his distance from the so–called mob in order to gain its respect is as much to blame as the coward who hides from his enemy because he fears to be defeated." Werther considers himself superior to the peasants he draws and converses with; they are like a spoiled boy's playthings, valued for their charming, poetic ignorance, useful because they offer Werther opportunities to feel liberal and wise. This example and several others, including the whole of the letter of May 22, suggest a lurking misanthropy beneath Werther's romantic facade, which will become more prevalent as the novel continues.

Analysis

Summary and Analysis of Book One: Letters of June 16–July 26

Summary

In the two and a half weeks since Werther's last letter, he has fallen in love. Indeed, he is so madly infatuated that he cannot even sit down long enough to write about it; he interrupts his letter to pay his beloved a visit, only afterwards sitting down to fill Wilhelm in on the events that have transpired. It seems that he met Bailiff S.'s daughter, Lotte, and she turned out to be the woman of his dreams. Her mother died several years before, and she has been selflessly caring for her younger brothers and sisters ever since.

Werther meets Lotte on the way to a dance. His first impression of her is as a mother, tending to her children. Her cheerfulness, her handsome appearance, grace, and charm all strike him immediately, and Lotte is instantly familiar with Werther, telling her siblings to call him "Uncle." As they drive to the dance, they discuss literature and discover that they both enjoy the sentimental fiction coming out of England, such as *The Vicar of Wakefield*. While at the dance, Lotte and Werther discover that they are perfectly suited to dancing together as well. Werther learns – much to his distress – that Lotte is engaged to a man named Albert. A storm breaks out, mirroring the turmoil in Werther's spirit, and in order to stave off fear the company at the dance gathers together, at Lotte's bidding, to play a parlor game. Werther is smitten, to say the least.

Werther begins to pay Lotte frequent visits at her hunting lodge. He moves to Wahlheim so that he can always be near her. Werther plays with her young siblings as though they are his own, extolling the virtues of family and children, and accompanies her on her visits about the region. On one such visit, to the village of St. —, Werther and Lotte fall in with the company of Herr Schmidt and Friederike. Werther berates Herr Schmidt for his gloomy disposition, claiming to hate nothing so much as a bad–humored person. Later, Lotte is engaged to visit Frau M., a woman in the town, while she is on her death bed. Everyone, it seems, loves Lotte and desires her company while facing life's darkest moments.

Lotte's feelings for Werther are decidedly ambiguous. Lotte is obviously fond of Werther, though she does not abandon herself to him the way he does to her. Lotte's feelings for Werther are never clarified, though Werther thinks that she begins to give him sympathetic looks, and often plays the clavichord to work off the tension (or the awkwardness) of their visits. Werther, meanwhile, says that he is happier than he has ever been during these days when he visits Lotte. He attempts to commemorate his happiness by sketching her, but cannot do so to his satisfaction, and instead settles for an image of her silhouette.

Meanwhile, the voice of Wilhelm creeps into the narrative, suggesting that Werther dedicate himself to drawing if that's his reason for staying in Wahlheim or, alternatively, that Werther take a position under the envoy. Wilhelm himself promises to secure this position for Werther. Werther seems dismissive of the opportunity for now.

Analysis

These are Werther's happiest days, and it is crucial to recognize how near Werther's happiness is to despair. When Lotte grants Werther's request to visit her again, he writes, "Since then, sun, moon, and stars may continue on their course; for me there is neither day nor night, and the entire universe about me has ceased to exist." This, somewhat surprisingly, is Werther's way of expressing passionate happiness; the reader must be forgiven for confusing this passage with a description of suicide.

These two valences, joy and despair, are knit together in everything Werther does. When he berates Herr Schmidt for his gloomy moods, Werther works up such a passion against bad humor that he ironically sends himself into a choleric fury. He writes, "How Lotte scolded me on the way home for my too warm sympathy with everything, saying it would be my ruin and that I should spare myself! O angel, for your sake I must live!" Once again, he ends his description of rapturous joy with a hint of suicide.

Like so many people who lack stability in their own lives, Werther cherishes Lotte's grounded sensibility. He is hugely invested in her maternal role, seeing her as an ideal, nourishing woman. Throughout Western literature, there has been an obsession with the impossible ideal of the virgin mother. Lotte's unique circumstances—being the oldest child in her family, temperamentally suited to child–rearing, and having a mother who died and left her in charge—allow this ancient fantasy of the virgin mother to be fulfilled. Lotte is a virgin mother, at once pure and sensual. She, like the Virgin Mary, plays an intercessional role in her community; the dying Frau M., for example, wants Lotte by her side while she dies.

Of course, Werther's role in Lotte's family is that of an outsider. He observes and participates in their daily functions, but he doesn't belong to them, and they – much as he may want them to – don't belong to him. Indeed, in the July 6 letter, Werther enthusiastically kisses Lotte's youngest sister, trying to express his love for her candor, and she bursts out screaming. Lotte placates her with a quasi–baptismal ritual. Werther can admire Lotte's skill with the children and can theorize about the blessedness of children and the wonder of Lotte's motherliness, but he cannot give a child a hug without scaring her half to death. Similarly, Werther stumbles over his own boots while dancing with Lotte, demonstrating his painful lack of poise. Later, in his letter of July 26 (one of the few letters not addressed to Wilhelm), Werther writes to Lotte, "No more sand in the notes you write me. I took today's too quickly to my lips, and something gritted between my teeth." Werther, the nature lover, gets sand in his teeth. For someone so passionately attached to the natural world, physical reality seems to confound Werther at every possible opportunity.

In this section, there are plenty of indications that things will not continue so happily for Werther. Perhaps the most telling moment in this second section of letters occurs when Werther tries to draw Lotte's portrait, but soon gives up and settles for her silhouette. Of course this conforms to Werther's aesthetic theory – that beauty is best captured in its natural, "artless" energy – but it also hints at the arrival of Albert, who will claim Lotte as his wife. Werther will indeed have to settle for her shadow.

Analysis

Summary and Analysis of Book One: Letters of June 30–September 10

Summary

Lotte's fiancé Albert arrives (he has been attending business following the death of his father and also applying for an official position) and Werther determines to leave. Werther likes Albert; he just cannot stand to see him "in possession of so much perfection." Werther reports that he esteems Albert for his "composure," contrasting with his own "inner restlessness," and indicates that Albert also admires him.

Werther's determination to leave is short lived, and without explanation we find that he is remaining in Wahlheim, visiting with Albert and Lotte together almost every night. Albert tells Werther of the virtue of Lotte's deceased mother, whose place she has filled perfectly, and they cultivate a friendship of their own, complementary to Werther's bond with Lotte. Albert provides Werther with a well-matched debate partner; on the occasion of borrowing Albert's hunting pistols, they argue about suicide, with Werther contending that suicide can be an act of absolute freedom and Albert arguing that no one capable of a larger view of life can be excused for committing suicide.

Confronted with the constant spectacle of Lotte and Albert's happiness, yet at the same time drawn to Lotte, her family, and even to Albert, Werther descends into misery. We learn through Werther's responses that Wilhelm is attempting to convince Werther to apply for the position at the Legation under Count C in order to escape an impossible situation. Meanwhile, the friendship between Lotte, Albert and Werther grows stronger; for his birthday, Albert gives Werther one of the pink ribbons Lotte was wearing when they first met and Lotte gives Werther a duodecimo copy of Homer.

Unable to resolve his love for Lotte with mere friendship, Werther applies for the position at the Legation and leave the company of Lotte and Albert. During his last visit with Lotte and Albert, while Albert and she are unaware that he is to leave so soon, they have an intense conversation about Lotte's deceased mother. At the end of this talk, Lotte says farewell as though they will meet again the next day. Werther collapses in grief with the knowledge that he cannot stand to be near the one he loves any longer.

Analysis

Werther's initial response to Albert's arrival is to leave—and it would have been wise for him to do so, in retrospect—but, without any explanation other than his "inner restlessness," he stays. For a brief month, Albert, Lotte and he achieve something of a balance: the love triangle works, because each member in it respects the others. Albert is a very good man – too sensible perhaps for Werther's taste, but a good friend nonetheless. He speaks, in a way, for Wilhelm (and, it will come to be clear, for the sensibility of the editor), and might be a great friend to Werther were it not for Lotte.

Some of the major themes of the novel gain clarity and force in this section. Werther's self–knowledge, for instance, begins to take on a tragic sheen. He writes of his impossible love for Lotte, "How clearly I have seen my condition, yet how childishly I have acted. How clearly I still see it, and yet show no sign of improvement." In this distinction between self–knowledge and self–satisfaction, Werther articulates his romantic disposition. Enlightenment thinkers might be inclined to equate self–knowledge with self–realization. Descartes' *cogito, ergo sum* places the onus of ego squarely on the thinker, implying that reason is the realm of the self. Ben Franklin, in his *Autobiography*, implies that acting virtuously is simply a matter of recognizing the right from the wrong in a given choice and choosing the right. Werther, in contrast, says that no matter how well he knows what he should do (for instance, "I should leave now that Albert has arrived"), his heart will ultimately steer his course, for better or worse. Werther recognizes the contradictions in his being, but rather than seeing them as problematic, sees them as definitional. This tendency is pure Romanticism.

Werther's inability to acknowledge his inherent contradictions lie at the root of his discontent. The passing references to suicide in earlier sections become central during this month, as Werther describes suicide as an example of an act in which reason has failed to satisfy the self, and passion must therefore take over. Of course, in his debate with Albert, Werther is speaking on a very personal level. He is quite comfortable with his suicidal tendencies. In speaking in defense of suicide he is not upholding an abstract cause, but is rather defending himself. Werther's right to suicide is, in many ways, the basis of his own being. He reserves the right to end his own life if he should ever need to. In this opinion, Werther draws from the ancient Romans; Pliny the Elder, for instance, in his *Natural History*, states that the ability to free oneself from the miseries of existence is what separates man from animal.

Now, however, is not Werther's time to kill himself, however unhappy he may be. He takes his leave from Albert and Lotte in what we might call a remarkably unselfish way. He reaches his limit, and simply leaves. Lotte's rumination at the end of Book One about her beloved mother and her expressed conviction that they will meet again in the next world is especially poignant given that (unbeknownst to her) Werther will never see her again. Her hope speaks for him, that in the next world they might at last be together. In this world, it is impossible.

Summary and Analysis of Book Two: Letters of October 20–March 24

Summary

A month and ten days have passed since Werther left Walheim when we next hear from him. It is unclear how he has spent his last month, but as of October 20 he has arrived at his place of official employment.

Werther begins his official tenure with hesitant optimism: he pledges to bear the tests of his new life as well as he can. On the plus side, Werther gets along splendidly with Count C.; on the minus, he is intensely annoyed by his immediate superior, the envoy. The envoy is a fact–happy and fussy man – Werther's opposite in spirit. On top of this natural enmity, the envoy becomes jealous of Count C.'s liking for Werther.

Another source of annoyance for Werther is the strict social code of his new town of employment. The aristocracy in the region meticulously cultivates its superiority, holding on to social privilege at all costs. Werther makes the acquaintance of Fräulein von B., a "charming creature" of aristocratic birth, whom he finds to be of sympathetic mind; his visits with Fräulein von B. are tarnished, however, by the presence of the young woman's old aunt, who is an intractable snob.

This local obsession with etiquette, manners and social niceties wears quickly on Werther. He feels as though his spirit is abandoning him. A week of stormy weather provides Werther with some respite, prompting him to write to Lotte about the miseries of his official position, as well as about his friendship with Fräulein von B. For the most part, however, Werther becomes increasingly impatient with the people and the customs that he must tolerate as part of his job.

Meanwhile, Werther's difficulties with the envoy increase. The envoy complains about his passionate methods to the Court Minister, who reproves Werther but then writes him a kind and understanding letter. On top of this, Werther learns in a letter from Albert that Lotte and he have been married. They have kept the wedding a secret from him, for which Werther thanks them.

While reeling from the news of Lotte and Albert's marriage, a further misfortune prompts Werther to resign from his post. Count C. invites Werther to dine on an evening when the local aristocracy is used to gathering at the Count's home. After dinner, the Count and Werther converse together as the aristocracy slowly begins to assemble. Werther does not take any notice, and before he knows it, almost all of the nobility have arrived. They all – even Fräulein von B. – act coldly toward him, and Werther realizes that something is amiss; however, he does not leave until Count C. himself asks him to.

The next day, there are local rumors about how the arrogant Werther was "snubbed." Werther is thoroughly humiliated by this gossip. He approaches Fräulein von B. and asks her why she treated him so coldly at the party; she tearfully replies that she was told to act that way by her aristocratic friends, and furthermore, that her aunt has lectured her against seeing him. This is the last straw for Werther, who sends in his resignation to the Court. He thus abandons his promising start in law and, he says, dooms his mother to disappointment in her son. Meanwhile, he has a plan for the next leg of his journey: Prince —, who likes Werther very much, has offered him lodging on his estates, and Werther has accepted the offer.

Analysis

The beginning of Book Two is, in many ways, a mirror image of Book One. Their settings are opposite: Book One is set in a rural region where Werther is the social equal or superior to all he meets; Book Two begins amongst the aristocracy, where Werther suddenly finds himself the low man on the totem pole. Werther himself has not fundamentally changed between the two books; he is still passionate, impulsive, and inwardly restless. He despises the meticulousness of the envoy with the same spirit that mocked the learning of V. or the practicality of Albert. Werther is still Werther, although his circumstances have changed – in some ways, perhaps, for the better, as he is no longer constantly reminded of his impossible situation with Albert and Lotte. Overall, however, it is clear that Werther cannot survive in the official environment of these letters.

Werther takes the job at court to escape from the irresolvable emotional triangle he has found himself in with Lotte and Albert, and from the looks of his letters, Werther makes a noble attempt at moving on. He writes one letter to Lotte, while holed up in a rustic inn during a winter storm, and one letter to Albert after hearing of their marriage. Aside from these brief attempts at correspondence, he makes no mention of his erstwhile friends. However, Werther's happiness is still defined in terms of Lotte – he makes his new friend, Fräulein von B., "pay homage" to her memory. He has escaped from his rustic, poetic, turbulent existence with Albert and Lotte into a nearly opposite existence among the cultured and the noble, but in so doing he has also escaped any chance of true happiness, however problematic such happiness may have been. He writes to Lotte that a reminder of her was his "first happy moment in a long time."

This unsuccessful attempt to find happiness away from Wahlheim is mirrored by an attempt to see whether his natural proclivity toward passion and sentiment is reconcilable with a respectable career. Whereas Werther seems doomed to long for Wahlheim, this second question is more ambiguous. He finds a great deal of success at the Court, winning the favor of the influential Count C. as well as the quieter admiration of the Court Minister. However, no matter how vociferously Werther commits himself to "hard work," it seems that he cannot abide a situation in which his intelligence and heart must take a backseat to questions of convention and class. Moreover, Werther is not one to compromise, and the world of law is built on compromise. He finds his spirit stifled by this atmosphere – a feeling that he often expresses, and which we can also observe in the infrequency of his letters during his time under the Minister. Werther has been sapped of passion, and thus the receptacles of his passion, his letters, have suffered as well.

The question of class is preeminent in these letters. Compare Werther's letter of May 15, 1771, where he writes of the lower classes, "I know quite well that we are not and cannot ever be equal," with his letter of December 24, 1771, when he writes, "I know…how necessary class distinctions are, and how many advantages I myself gain from them; but they should not stand in my way just when I might enjoy some little pleasure, some gleam of joy on this earth." In the first case, Werther somewhat patronizingly stands on his privilege, while in the second he learns the limits of that privilege. In Book One, Werther's class status works for him; in Book Two, however, it works against him, and it is his "snubbing" by the upper classes that ostensibly drives him away.

A word about Werther's resignation: W.H. Auden, who is of the opinion that Werther is an egocentric monster, and that Goethe intended us to see him that way, cites Werther's resignation as the preeminent example of his selfishness. He writes,

> If a man thinks the social conventions of his time and place to be
> silly or wrong, there are two courses of behavior that will earn him
> an outsider's respect. Either he may keep his opinions to himself
> and observe the conventions with detached amusement, or he may
> deliberately break them for the pleasure of the shock he
> causes…Werther, by staying on [at the party] when it is clear that
> his presence is unwelcome, defies the company, but his precious
> ego is hurt by their reactions, and he resigns from his post, returns
> to Lotte and disaster for all.

It is certainly true that Werther's behavior at the party seems inconsistent with his subsequent indignation – and perhaps we want to agree with Auden that Werther is a demanding and fiercely egocentric young man. There is, however, a tragic, subtle upshot to Werther's restless actions: Werther knows himself incredibly well; he knows his own follies and foibles; but this self-knowledge never helps him. His passions rule his actions, whatever he may think. If Werther's actions seem inconsistent and lunatic, so be it, but remember that no one knows this better than Werther himself.

Analysis

Summary and Analysis of Book Two: Letters of April 19–December 6

Summary

After Werther's resignation from the court is accepted, he travels to his place of birth en route to the Prince's estates. He writes of his joy at seeing the old landmarks of his childhood, and his disdain at seeing new additions to the landscape. Once settled with the Prince, Werther claims at first that things are going well, but very quickly grows tired of conversing with his host. He admits that he "only want[s] to be closer to Lotte once more," though he is chilled by the thought of her marriage to Albert, and makes plans to relocate back to Wahlheim.

On his way back to Wahlheim, Werther meets two of his past acquaintances. First, he meets the mother of Hans and Philip, who tells him tragic news: Hans has died, and her husband has returned from Switzerland without receiving any money. Further along, Werther runs into the country lad who loved his widow employer. Tragedy has struck in this quarter as well: the country lad, unable to stand his love any longer, made overtures to the widow, who resisted him. The country lad was inclined to rape her in his madness, when the widow's brother showed up and drove him out of the house. Now, the lad says, his place has been filled by another worker, and he is filled with intense jealousy.

Once settled again in Wahlheim, Werther tries to reestablish his friendship with Lotte, though he is more and more dangerously drawn to her. His lack of physical contact with Lotte becomes an obsession. Lotte, who is still fond and trusting of Werther, ambiguously abets his growing madness. For instance, she has a small bird who kisses Werther's mouth and then her own. Meanwhile, Wahlheim, too, is not the rustic paradise Werther once took it for. The new pastor's wife, in her disregard for nature, has cut down the local walnut trees; Werther is incensed by this loss.

Befitting Werther's increasingly turbulent spirit, Homer has been replaced in his esteem by Ossian, the legendary poet of Scotland. Werther's thoughts are constantly occupied by death and suicide – even more so than before. Complementing these thoughts of death are frequent thoughts of sex. He desires Lotte as he never has before, and feels himself drifting into madness. Ossian and religion are his only consolations – and religion becomes an increasingly ambiguous, incomprehensible force in Werther's life.

A chance meeting represents all of Werther's fear and despair: while taking a walk in the winter weather, he comes across Heinrich, a man "in a shabby green coat" who is acting strangely. Werther discovers that the man is searching for wildflowers because "he has promised his sweetheart a nosegay." Heinrich carries on about a past time when he was well–off, and curses his current existence. This madman's mother comes along and tells Werther that this idealized past Heinrich talks about is in fact the time he spent in the asylum, "when he did not know himself." Werther is tossed into despair by this thought. To top all, Albert later tells Werther that Heinrich was once an employee of Lotte's father, and had developed an impossible passion for her. When he confessed his love, he was dismissed from his job and went insane.

Haunted beyond reason by his need for Lotte, Werther reaches new depths of suffering. He feels his fate linked to the other unfortunates in this section – Heinrich and the country lad with a passion for the widow – and even wishes for Albert's death when he is not wishing for his own. The editor takes up Werther's story while he flounders in the depths of desolation.

Analysis

One of the most titillating threads in *Werther* is the largely unexplained relationship between Werther and his mother – a relationship that doesn't receive much ink in the novel but which nonetheless informs a great deal of its action. This section begins with the most direct references to their relationship. In one letter, Werther writes that he "wont need the money from [his] mother, for which [he] asked her the other day" – implying that Werther remains financially dependent upon his mother. In the next letter, Werther writes about visiting the place of his birth, saying, "I plan to enter the town by the same gate through which my mother drove out with me when she left the dear familiar place after the death of my father to shut herself in the unbearable town where she now lives."

What should we make of this? First – and most obviously – Goethe reveals that Werther is on uneasy ground with his mother, and by extension his family as a whole. He depends on his mother financially, and yet he does not write her letters directly, instead relying on Wilhelm as a go–between. This uneasy relationship seems to stem from his mother's decision, following the death of his father, to move to whatever "unbearable town" Werther refers to. This unhappy experience with his own family seems to account for a great deal of Werther's instability. Though Lotte and her family are not mentioned in these specific letters, it makes sense that one who lost both his father and moved away from his rural birthplace at a young age would cling to Wahlheim as a sort of idyllic replacement. Werther is perhaps redirecting the love he denies to his mother to Lotte, whom he sees as a perfect motherly being. This becomes further complicated, of course, as Lotte becomes increasingly sexualized, which we also see happening in this section.

This sexualizing of Lotte is one of the major developments in the latter half of *Werther*. In the letter of September 12, Lotte and Werther undergo a strange courtship ritual when Lotte passes Werther a bird that has just pecked at her lips. She says, "'He shall kiss you too'…handing the bird over to me. The tiny beak made its way from her lips to mine, and the pecking touch was like a breath – a foretaste of the pleasures of love." This flirtation is odd, to be sure, but is captures Lotte and Werther's growing relationship: their connection, from the beginning, has been based on a romantic affinity with Nature – it is the only medium through which Lotte and Werther are allowed to share their love. The bird, as a representative of nature, symbolizes this connection. Furthermore, in Germanic folktale traditions, the bird is often depicted as a go–between in human courtships, a tradition that still resonates in more contemporary literature. On yet another level, birds have been used as phallic symbols since ancient Roman times. There are several famous poems by Catullus (accessible in the "related links" section of this analysis) that use birds in this manner, and Werther, learned man that he is, certainly knows his Catullus. The bird, of course, is just one instance of an intense, burgeoning need in Werther to consummate his love with Lotte (see, for example, the letter of November 22). This unsatisfied physical need, as much as anything, is what ultimately drives him to suicide.

Once Werther returns to Wahlheim, his miserable trajectory not only complicates his relationship with Lotte and Albert, but also contaminates the lives of the local peasants he once eulogized, and even the very landscape. Both young Hans and the country lad have met misfortune head–on; the loss of the walnut trees expresses the fall from grace of Wahlheim as a whole. In addition, Werther meets Heinrich, a ghoulish foreshadowing of the madness that Lotte's can inspire in a man. Werther seems most threatened by Heinrich's feeling that he was happiest when in an asylum, for Werther is obsessed with subjective knowledge; for him, it would be worse than death to be alive and ignorant, like Heinrich.

Werther's suffering eventually becomes so pronounced that language itself is insufficient to express it. From the beginning of the novel, Werther has been playfully fascinated with the limitations of expressive language; he remarks regularly that trite and tired phrases cannot capture the beauty of sentiment. See, for instance, his argument with Albert in the letter of August 12, or his letter of May 30, in which he describes the country lad's love for the widow. However, as the novel builds to its tragic end, prosaic language is not merely inadequate for Werther: he begins to feel that the only way of expressing himself is through terse, opaque epigrams (see the letters of June 16 and October 10). In the last days of his life, Werther loses the ability to express himself with words, and can only use dashes that seem loaded with the inexpressible burden of his sorrow. Werther's inability to put into language his growing misery is why the need for an editor becomes so obvious in the last section of the novel.

Analysis

Summary and Analysis of The Editor to the Reader

Summary

In the final section of the novel the editor steps in, informing us that he has taken great pains to discover the full history of Werther's final months both from documents and interviews. In the editor's narrative, Albert grows increasingly wary of Werther's visits. He begins to leave the room when Werther comes by, worried that this triangle is not being seen charitably by propriety. Werther does not take this hint, instead resenting Albert's conventionality; his conviction that Lotte would have been happier with him grows stronger. Lotte, caught in the middle, tries not to offend either her husband or her good friend, but begins to tire of Werther's intrusions.

While on a walk with Lotte, Werther hears that the country lad with whom he identifies has murdered his replacement in the widow's service. Werther attempts to plead for the country lad before the bailiff, explaining his motives; of course, the bailiff doesn't listen. During Werther's agony over this case, he writes a letter to Wilhelm stating that torrential rains, seemingly expressive of his turbulent soul, have flooded Wahlheim. Meanwhile, Werther grows more obsessed with Lotte: in a letter written on December 14, he states that, unable to control himself, he held her in his arms and covered her with kisses.

The editor writes that this concurrence of misfortune is what makes Werther decide to take his own life; he bides his time in doing so, however, until he can fully accept his decision and execute it with a calm hand. Lotte has also reached a determination of her own: she cannot continue to see Werther so frequently, given Albert's tacit disapproval. Three days before Christmas, when Werther visits her at night, Lotte tells him not to visit again until Christmas Eve; she tries to convince him to accept a new, conventional friendship with her, adding (with unimpeachable insight) that "it is only the impossibility of possessing [her] that attracts [Werther] so much." Werther, hopelessly distraught, retreats.

He begins to write a long suicide note addressed to Lotte, in which he determines that either he, Albert, or she must die, and he is resolved that it shall be himself. After beginning his letter, then settling his affairs, Werther – against Lotte's wishes – pays his beloved a final visit. When she hears him ask for her, Lotte tries to invite some of her friends over so she won't be alone with him (Albert is away on business), but the friends cannot come. Lotte and Werther find themselves in an incredibly uncomfortable situation, which Lotte tries to diffuse first by playing the clavichord, then by having Werther read from his translation of Ossian. This excerpt is very long. The Ossian sends Lotte and Werther into hysterics as "they [feel] their own misery in the fate of the noble Gaels." Unable to restrain himself, Werther forces a kiss between he and Lotte; furious, she orders him out of her house, never to see her again.

When at his home once again, after having taken a late–night hike in the pouring rain to relieve his spirit, Werther writes to Lotte, requesting Albert's hunting pistols. Albert, meanwhile, has returned, and assents to lending Werther the pistols. Lotte passes them to Werther's servant with her own hands. When Werther receives the pistols, delighted that Lotte has apparently implied approval of his suicidal intentions, he spends the rest of the evening going through his papers, burning some and preserving others. He addresses the final section to his suicide letter to Lotte, noting his wishes for burial and saying that his soul is at peace with his decision. Just after the stroke of midnight, he shoots himself in the head.

The shot does not immediately kill him. The next morning, Werther is found – the death–rattle in his throat – with his brain laid bare. The doctor tries to save him, but in vain. Lotte, Albert and her family attend his final hours. The novel closes: "That night around eleven the bailiff had Werther buried at the place he himself had chosen. The old man and his sons followed the body to the grave; Albert was unable to. Lotte's life was in danger. Workmen carried the coffin. No clergyman attended."

Analysis

There is plenty to unpack in this final section – every action is so loaded with meaning. We can examine Werther's suicide, during which his soul indeed seems to have finally found peace, as the normally excessive Werther requires only "one glass of wine" before pulling the trigger (reminding us of the letter of November 8, in which Lotte implores him not to drink "the whole bottle"). We can discuss about how appropriate it is that Albert is away "on business" when Werther pays his last visit to Lotte, proving to some extent Werther's point that Albert cares more about his office than his wife. We can mull over the reading of Ossian, which most critics agree is terribly inappropriate for a climactic scene, especially given its length and its opacity, but which we can see as a clear expression of the zeitgeist. *Sturm und Drang* relies on the knowingness of its initiates, of whom Lotte and Werther are two examples. Such authentic Romantics would not need context for Ossian – in fact they would scoff at those who do – and so Goethe doesn't provide any. His translation of Ossian is in this light an audacious gesture, like a stretch of feedback and free jazz at an *avant garde* rock show, intended to separate the true Romantics from the pretenders who don't get it. But what is most telling in the last section of *Werther*, perhaps, is the use of the editor.

Who is this editor? Who would take so much trouble to document, with "exact facts," the final days and hours of Werther's life? There have been many suggestions as to the identity of this editor, maybe the most creative being that it is Werther himself narrating from beyond the grave (and who but Werther would be so interested in himself?). The fact remains, however, that Goethe deliberately left the identity of the editor vague and impossible to determine.

What is more important about the editor is that he represents, to some degree at least, a refutation of Werther's philosophy. He is an organizer, a gatherer of facts, and a scientist of suffering, so to speak. The editor emphasizes the role that deliberation, not spontaneity (Werther's argument), plays into the forging of art. In his respectful attentiveness to Werther's motives and character, married to his gentle and implicit refutation of Werther's theory of art, the editor provides a model for the ideal reader of Werther: someone who appreciates the tumult and enthusiasm that Werther represents without letting that appreciation snowball into emulation. It seems to be the sensible voice of Goethe himself, who has lived through the turmoil that Werther experienced, but who comes to embrace some aspects of Enlightenment order, and represents an embedded critique of his own zealous creation. What a pity that the readers of the late eighteenth century took this book to be an unabashed endorsement of Werther's lifestyle, even to the point of copying his fate. (Needless to say, the irony is apparent: the "non-conformists" conforming to the fate of their hero, wearing his blue and yellow garb and scented, perhaps, with the popular perfume, *Eau de Werther...*)

At the final accounting, it is hard to say whether Werther is to be despised, or to be pitied for his fate, as the editor's note at the beginning of the novel implores us. Werther himself knows, especially in these final letters, that he seems doomed to bring unhappiness to those he loves most, but this self-knowledge cannot wholly vindicate the pain he brings both to Albert and Lotte's otherwise happy marriage; the novel ends, after all, with uncertainty as to whether or not Lotte will survive the shock of Werther's death. If he truly cared for Lotte – and if he were really as calm in his decision as he claims – shouldn't he have chosen a different location for the deed, sparing her the immediate sight of his dead body? Even his calmness is carefully staged: the single glass of wine, the open copy of Lessing.

It is worth noting, in the end, that Werther leaves the world in an utterly inelegant manner. His final Romantic gesture ends unromantically, with his messy, dying corpse. Goethe's style in this final section is anything but Romantic: he uses spare, short sentences, utterly factual and unsentimental. Of course the ending is moving – especially the last sentences, in which the themes of class (the workmen carry his coffin) and religion (he is denied a religious burial) are so concisely touched upon – but it is ambiguous as to whether or not it offers an endorsement of Werther's dire decision.

Analysis

Suggested Essay Questions

1. What does Goethe think about Werther? Is his protagonist a brilliant enthusiast of emotionalism, a self–absorbed villain, or something in between? Use textual evidence in making your case.

2. What are your impressions of Wilhelm? Although he doesn't speak for himself in *Werther*, he is a constant presence simply in being addressed. What is Wilhelm like, and who else in the novel is like him?

3. Discuss the women in *Werther*. What is Werther's opinion of the ideal woman? What qualities does she possess? Does Goethe agree with Werther, or is there some distance between them on this issue?

4. What is the role of class in the novel? Who is high class, who is low class, and where does Werther fit in this schema? Describe his attitude toward the lower classes.

5. Discuss the sideplots of *Werther*, especially focusing on the story of the country lad and the widowed employer whom he loves.

6. Madness is a lurking force in *Werther*. Who in the novel is mad? What is the meaning of madness in the novel?

7. Why is the editor a part of *Werther*? How does his or her presence influence the novel? What does it mean for *Werther* to have been edited, and how should the reader respond to this fact?

8. Is Werther good with children? What role does he play in his relationships with them? What is his opinion of them?

9. Discuss Werther's relationship with his mother. Werther never addresses her directly and seems to have a strained relationship with her; for instance, she doesn't even hear about his death at the novel's end, let alone attend the funeral (which takes place nowhere near her). Find textual clues as to the nature of this relationship. Why isn't she a focal point of the novel – or is she?

10. What is Werther's attitude toward learning? Is it as simple as he represents it?

Suggested Essay Questions

Sturm und Drang

Goethe is often cited as one of the first proponents of the *Sturm und Drang* movement. In essence, {Sturm und Drang is a German literary and musical movement that emphasizes intense subjectivity. "Sturm und Drang" literally means "storm and urge," though it's often translated "storm and stress." The name captures the two main aspects of *Sturm und Drang* art: first, "storm" emphasizes the role of nature's sublime power in inspiring the artist; second, "urge" or "stress" emphasizes the role of the emotions or the will in expressing the turmoil present in nature.

The *Sturm und Drang* movement emerged in Germany as a reaction against the Enlightenment – and as such, it is an important precursor to Romanticism. *Sturm und Drang* artists emphasized the limits of reason, believing that while man is capable of knowing the difference between right and wrong, his emotional nature may compel him to act irrationally. Instead of seeing this irrational urge as problematic, as Enlightenment thinkers tended to do, the *Sturm und Drang* movement sees it as the defining characteristic of a human being. A human being is most human, it holds, when she or he acts in accordance with unhindered emotions.

The term *Sturm und Drang* comes from the title of a play written in 1776 by Friedrich Maximilian Klinger (1752–1831). However, the essence of the genre existed before Klinger's play gave it a name. German poets and philosophers such as Heinrich Wilhelm von Gerstenberg (1737–1823), Johann Georg Hamann (1730–1788), and Johann Gottfried Herder (1744–1803) were important precursors of Goethe in developing the vocabulary of *Sturm und Drang*. Yet it was Goethe and his friend, the playwright, poet and philosopher Friedrich Schiller (1759–1805), who brought the genre to its richest and most enduring expression. *The Sorrows of Young Werther*, without a doubt, is the *Sturm und Drang* work that most defines the genre today. In music, the minor key symphonies that Franz Joseph Haydn composed in the 1770s, such as his Symphony no. 45 ("The Farewell"), are lasting examples of the *Sturm und Drang* sensibility.

It is important not to collapse *Sturm und Drang* under the canopy of Romanticism. The former certainly influenced the latter – and might even be considered a sub–genre of the latter – but only in the same way that the minor key symphonies of Haydn and Mozart influenced the unquestionably Romantic works of Beethoven and Berlioz. In literature, *Sturm und Drang* is closer to the Enlightenment sensibility than its proponents may have been comfortable admitting. *Werther*, for instance, is a meticulously composed work that ultimately casts its protagonist's excesses in ambiguity. Goethe and Schiller both, for their parts, moved away from *Sturm und Drang* after visiting Italy. They ended up espousing Weimar Classicism, a rationalist aesthetic, and backing away from the passionate works of their youths. In short, one can sense Classical elements in *Sturm und Drang*, just as one can sense elements of *Sturm und Drang* in the Classical movement.

Author of ClassicNote and Sources

W.C. Miller, author of ClassicNote. Completed on May 31, 2006, copyright held by GradeSaver.

Updated and revised Jordan Berkow June 14, 2006. Copyright held by GradeSaver.

Johann Wolfgang von Goethe, Trans. Elizabeth Mayer and Louise Bogan. The Sorrows of Young Werther. New York: Vintage, 1990.

Goethe, Trans. Catherine Hutter. "Reflections on Werther". New York: Signet Books, 1962.

Goethe, Trans. Catherine Hutter. "Goethe in Sesenheim". New York: Signet Books, 1962.

Bruce Duncan. Goethe's Werther and the Critics. New York: Camden House, 2005.

Thomas Carlyle. The Sorrows of Young Werther: Criticism and Interpretation. Cambridge: Harvard University Press, 1917.

"Wikipedia." 2006–05–30. <http://en.wikipedia.org/>.

"Merriam–Webster Online." 2006–05–30. <http://www.m–w.com/>.

"The Dictionary of Sensibility." 2006–05–30. <http://www.engl.virginia.edu/enec981/dictionary/intro.html>.

Essay: Werther As a Force of Nature

by Janet Rosenbaum
March 14, 1997

From the beginning of The Sorrows of Young Werther, Werther emphasizes his connection to Nature in order to embellish the tragically creative persona he presents to Wilhelm. As his infatuation with Charlotte grows and he laments the injustice and misfortune of his situation, his views distort; we see his self–perceived affinity with Nature becoming more twisted and less peaceful. A turning point in this tranformation can be seen in his entry of 18 August; Nature is no longer sublime and beautiful to him, but merely sublime and filled with the potential for destruction: Werther finds himself paralyzed by the thoughts of his own destructive powers.

Werther is describing the anguish of his unrequited love for Charlotte, which has transformed his previous love for Nature into torment. The extent of his torment is described in the form of a vision: â œIt is as if a curtain had been drawn from before my eyes,â ? hinting at an epiphany–changed Werther, expecting to feel attachment and oneness with Nature, but â œinstead of prospects of eternal life, the abyss of an ever–open grave yawned before me.â ? The image of a curtain being drawn aside to reveal a Truth which concerns â œthe prospects of eternal lifeâ ? has strongly religious connotations; despite its lack of precision, this phrase conveys a wealth of images associated with ineffable experiences as in Biblical stories of religious epiphanies; curtains are prominent in Old Testament descriptions of the ark and the Holy of Holies ––– where a curtain encloses the heavenly presence. Such a religious tone indicates that Werther views this revelation with the fervency of a prophet, willing to allow it to determine his fate.

Inflated imagery dominates the rest of the paragraph: Werther finds himself overshadowed by storms, torrents, the ocean, time, and Nature, the â œall–comsuming monster.â ? These parallel his fear of his own destructive power: that at some scale he, too, is all–consuming, and could destroy a world in the same way an earthquake swallows a village.

Werther finds himself before â œthe abyss of an ever–open grave,â ? which symbolises to Werther the tenuousness of his life: that he might plunge into the abyss as easily as falling into a hole in the ground. While a grave is a clear connection between this world and the next, an abyss is of a completely different category.\footnote{Abyss, in its original sense, means â œan other–worldly pit,â ? in contrast to the weaker modern connotation.} That Werther can magnify one into the other gives this paragraph a fantastic flavour: in Werther's dreams and visions an earthly grave becomes otherworldly and grows in magnititude when he interprets it.

Werther continues with this image of life's tenuousness: â œCan we say of anything that it is when all passes away?â ? Werther's question is more clearly emphatic in the German: â œKannst du sagen: Das ist! da alles vor ubergeht?â ? One can picture Werther standing at the edge of his abyss shouting these words at the turbulent grey sky, in the sort of stereotypical angst–ridden soliloquy he would, no doubt, enjoy giving.

Imagery of blindly consuming forces bolsters this image, as Werther expounds upon existence's ephemerality: â œCan we say of anything than it is when all passses away ––– when time, with the speed of a storm, carries all things onward ––– and our transitory existence, hurried along by the torrent, is swallowed up by the waves or dashed against the rocks?â ?

Although Werther changes metaphors for this fateful natural power three times in the course of the sentence, the image of coursing water, relentless in its flow, is explicit in each: time is compared with storms, torrents, and ocean waves ––– a human may be carried away by time, like a sapling may be uprooted and carried away by coursing water. The imagery of rushing water parallels that of the sentence itself: although the sentence is long, its flowing nature ––– especially its many dependent clauses ––– and common imagery carry the reader to finish the sentence before realising that the metaphor for time changed several times midcourse. The image of being swallowed by such forces is also introduced in this sentence ––– the waves are of such enormousness (and enormity!) that they could simply engulf one's existence and extinguish it. In some sense, one could see a beginning of the swallowing motif in the vision of the abyss, which is sometimes described as engulfing humans in older poetry and literature.

In accord with this swallowing motif, Werther concludes, â œThere is not a moment that doesn't consume you and yours ––– not a moment in which you don't yourself destroy something.â ? The first part of this sentence continues the theme of time as an active force; that time could consume a person inverts the usual image of humans as consumers of time; one is literally eaten by each moment which elapses. Thus, Werther's imagery evolves: instead of merely being caught in the flow of time, one is consumed by each sucessive moment in what might be seen as a perverse game of Pacman.

The second half of the phrase reveals an interesting leap of logic; Werther concludes that because each person is consumed/destroyed, each must also consume and destroy. While it's possible that Werther has simply jumped to conclusions, brooding about the destructive power of Nature, and concluding that he, as part of Nature, must also be inherently destructive, a more plausible conclusion is that Werther has imagined a world on a smaller scale, for which he is a large force. This alternate interpretation evokes the initial scene when he observes â œthe little world among the stalksâ ? (6), and finds himself so entranced with the insects and plants on such a small scale.

In fact, Werther shows his concern for such small worlds: â œThe most innocent walk costs thousands of poor insects their lives; one step destroys the delicate structures of the ant and turns a little world into chaos.â ?

Essay: The Sorrows of Young Werther: Passion vs. Rationality

by Anonymous
April 23, 2004

In "The Sorrows of Young Werther", by Goethe, one of the prevalent themes is the control that passion wields over one's actions. Passion may cause one to act irrationally, a belief that Goethe espoused despite the paradigm that dominated the society of his day: that man should allow rationality and common sense to control his life. The story takes place in Germany in 1771, and is written in epistolary form. The letters are composed by a lovesick man named Werther, destined to take his life because the object of his affection is married to another, and are addressed to a trusted friend named Wilhelm. Werther takes a romantic view on life, letting his heart and passions guide him. He sees death as a heroic escape, often favors imagination over reality, and hates the fact that the men of his time are mechanical, static conformists that allow so–called "common sense" to rule their decisions.

Passion and romantic ideals lead Werther down the path that will ultimately end in his demise. When speaking of a friend, Werther states that "he admires my intelligence and my talents more than my heart, which is, after all, my only pride, and the fountainhead of all – all strength, happiness and misery" (97). Because he lets his heart guide him, the misery he speaks of outweighs his strength and happiness. Werther lets his imagination take control of his mind more often than his common sense, yet another trait of romantics. He believes that one is happiest when under the spell of delusions, as can be seen when he writes of a woman described to him by a boy:

I shall try to see her as soon as possible, or rather, after giving it a second thought, I shall avoid her. It is better that I see her through the eyes of her lover; she might not appear to my own eyes, in reality, as I now see her; and why should I destroy the lovely image I already possess? (20)

Werther prefers an image, a picture existing solely in his head, to an uncertain reality.

It is his heart that Werther listens to, and his heart that he feels he must sacrifice. It appears, on the surface, that Goethe is reprimanding those who have the same perspective on life as Werther by murdering him at the end of the novel. It seems that those who oppose him are, in fact, "correct" in their actions.

Nearly every character in the novel, with few exceptions, subscribe to classical ideals and dogmas. Classicists, the opposite of romantics, favor uniformity, common sense, rationality, and the mind over romantic ideas. Throughout the book, Werther's friends demand that he gain some common sense: Wilhelm writes, "pull yourself together and try to get rid of an unfortunate passion that is bound to burn up all your energy" (54). Wilhelm tries to convince Werther to toss aside his passion, the very emotion on which he thrives. Wilhelm is aware that should Werther continue to live with such passion in his life, his energy will soon be spent. Even Lotte, the woman Werther loves and lives for, hopes that he will turn away from his irrationality:

Werther! You can, you must see us again; only do be reasonable. Oh, why did you have to be born with this violent temper, this uncontrollable clinging passion for everything you touch! Please...be reasonable! Your intellect, your knowledge, your talents, should offer you such a variety of satisfactions! (138)

The word "reasonable" is repeated to emphasize the way that Werther should be, according to the classical ideals of the time. Lotte speaks of intellect and knowledge, both of which are basic facets of classicism. Knowledge is based on facts, and facts are unchanging, solid, and static; these are traits that Werther's friends try to impose on him throughout the book. However, Goethe is not trying to encourage people to embrace the classical outlook on life. Although it may appear so, he is in fact doing just the opposite; into Werther's suicide, Goethe weaves heroism, sympathy, and honor.

Throughout his life, Werther has been urged to embrace rationality and think things through. Ultimately, however, he realizes that he cannot control his passions; to the contrary, his passions control him. Werther meets another like him, who cannot control himself either: "his passion for the woman...had daily grown on him, to the degree that he finally had not known what to do...He had not been able to eat, to drink or sleep; he had felt as if something was choking him(103)." Werther, too, feels as if some higher force is controlling his actions. Werther is not punished for letting his passion rule him; he takes his life, and this is what he has longed for more than anything. He welcomes death with open arms: he "shuddered with awe and also with longing" (133). Werther's death is heroic, at least in his eyes; this is proven when he reads from some songs of Ossian to Lotte. He says, "Tall thou art on the hill; fair among the sons of the vale. But thou shalt fall like Morar; the mourner shall sit on thy tomb" (149). He envisions his own death as similarly heroic, with Lotte weeping for him atop his grave, because he was brave enough to take his own life. He argues profusely with Albert, Lotte's husband, when Albert says that suicide is weak: "For it is certainly easier to die than bravely to bear a life of misery" (59). Werther never changes his view on this subject, believing that suicide is grand.

Goethe also uses the epistolary form to glorify Werther's death. It is common for heroes to be described as god–like, immortal, and impervious. Because the letters show the passage of time and end with Werther's death, Werther is dropped to the rank of a mere mortal. However, he is still a hero, and the fact that his death is imminent only suggests that he is normal: an everyman hero. In this mannner, readers are encouraged to relate to Werther, and to embrace his romantic ideas.

Though "The Sorrows of Young Werther" appears to praise the classical outlook on life, a closer reading reveals that Goethe is, to the contrary, espousing the romantic view. It is the classical element in those around Werther that kills him, for none of his friends can stand the fact that he has let his heart guide him through life. His death touches those close to them, despite their many differences. It is passion that rules Werther: he can do nothing to appease his heart, and must ultimately accept that perhaps this is simply how life is.

Quiz 1

1. **Before writing The Sorrows of Young Werther, Goethe:**
    A. Wrote a tragedy based on the life of Götz von Berlichingen
    B. Unsuccussfully attempted suicide
    C. Was a poor laborer
    D. Traveled to Italy and wrote a memoir of the experience

2. **The Sorrows of Young Werther is:**
    A. An epistolatory novel
    B. A narrative poem
    C. An autobiography
    D. A burlesque

3. **Werther was first published in:**
    A. 1750
    B. 1774
    C. 1781
    D. 1800

4. **When was Goethe's revision of Werther published?**
    A. Posthumously
    B. 1810
    C. 1781
    D. 1777

5. **Which of the following ISN'T true of Goethe's revision of Werther?**
    A. It is the version widely read today
    B. It is the only version widely available in an English translation
    C. It emphasizes the editor's role in the narrative, compared to the original
    D. It is considerably more sympathetic to Werther's point of view than the original

6. **Werther is set in:**
    A. The 1680s
    B. 1774
    C. 1771–1772
    D. The South of France

7. Almost all of Werther's letters are addressed to:
   A. His friend, Albert
   B. His mother
   C. His beloved, Lotte
   D. His friend, Wilhelm

8. Who is Leonora?
   A. A statue that Werther considers the ideal feminine form
   B. Wilhelm's wife, about whom Werther inquires
   C. Werther's beloved
   D. A woman who was in love with Werther before the novel begins

9. Werther's family is:
   A. Largely divided by misunderstanding and neglect
   B. Proud of him
   C. Happy but stifling
   D. Almost all deceased

10. Werther compares the peasant women he sees at the well to:
   A. A ballad
   B. Children
   C. Women depicted in Homer
   D. Women in biblical times

11. As the novel begins, what is Werther's opinion of books?
   A. He asks Wilhelm to send his library to his new residence
   B. He is very fond of them
   C. He says that he needs none but his Homer
   D. He says he needs none at all

12. Werther finds the village of Wahlheim:
   A. Charming
   B. Stifling
   C. Provincial
   D. Dilapidated

13. Who are Hans and Philip?

    A. Werther's horses

    B. Lotte's two youngest siblings

    C. Werther's friends, with whom he attends a ball

    D. Two peasant brothers whom Werther sketches

14. What does Werther say he admires in a woman?

    A. Beauty

    B. Cheerfulness

    C. Intellect

    D. Physical strength

15. Bailiff S. is:

    A. The father of nine children

    B. The father of Hans and Philip

    C. The father of eight children

    D. Disagreeable to Werther

16. When Werther first sees Lotte, she is:

    A. Dancing with Albert at a ball

    B. Wearing a green dress

    C. Splashing in a duck pond

    D. Feeding her siblings bread

17. After Lotte, who is the oldest of the siblings?

    A. Hans

    B. Heike

    C. Louis

    D. Sophy

18. Who wrote The Vicar of Wakefield?

    A. Goethe

    B. Jean–Jaques Rousseau

    C. Oliver Goldsmith

    D. Samuel Richardson

19. **When Werther is dancing with Lotte he:**
    A. Stumbles
    B. Kisses her
    C. Winks at her
    D. Dances flawlessly

20. **Werther's first meeting with Lotte is interrupted by:**
    A. Albert
    B. His jealous partner
    C. A thunderstorm
    D. A musical recital

21. **Who is Klopstock?**
    A. A German philosopher
    B. A German artist
    C. A German composer
    D. A German poet

22. **What is Werther's attitude toward Lotte's brothers and sisters?**
    A. He thinks that they are selfish with Lotte's time
    B. He considers them to be lovely models for the rest of humanity
    C. He is pedantic toward them, teaching them to read and write
    D. He secretly dislikes them

23. **Lotte is asked:**
    A. To call off her engagement with Albert
    B. To leave for Austria with Albert
    C. To bake bread for the parishioners of Wahlheim
    D. To attend a dying woman's deathbed

24. **Who does Werther berate for submitting to bad moods?**
    A. Albert
    B. Herr Schmidt
    C. Lotte
    D. Friedericke

25. **What is Lotte's response to Werther's attack on bad moods?**
    A. She scolds him for sympathizing too warmly with everything
    B. She says that he should write a pamphlet on the subject and promulgate his opinion
    C. She praises his judgement and expression
    D. She is thrown into a bad mood herself

Quiz 1 Answer Key

1. (**A**) Wrote a tragedy based on the life of Götz von Berlichingen
2. (**A**) An epistolary novel
3. (**B**) 1774
4. (**C**) 1781
5. (**D**) It is considerably more sympathetic to Werther's point of view than the original
6. (**C**) 1771–1772
7. (**D**) His friend, Wilhelm
8. (**D**) A woman who was in love with Werther before the novel begins
9. (**A**) Largely divided by misunderstanding and neglect
10. (**D**) Women in biblical times
11. (**C**) He says that he needs none but his Homer
12. (**A**) Charming
13. (**D**) Two peasant brothers whom Werther sketches
14. (**B**) Cheerfulness
15. (**A**) The father of nine children
16. (**D**) Feeding her siblings bread
17. (**D**) Sophy
18. (**C**) Oliver Goldsmith
19. (**A**) Stumbles
20. (**C**) A thunderstorm
21. (**D**) A German poet
22. (**B**) He considers them to be lovely models for the rest of humanity
23. (**D**) To attend a dying woman's deathbed
24. (**B**) Herr Schmidt
25. (**A**) She scolds him for sympathizing too warmly with everything

Quiz 2

1. **How does Werther frighten Lotte's youngest sister?**
    A. He pours water over her head
    B. He jumps out from around a corner of the hunting lodge
    C. He lifts her up and fervently kisses her
    D. He tells her a story about a Princess served by ghostly hands

2. **How does Lotte console her sister after Werther scares her?**
    A. She has the little girl wash her face in the spring water
    B. She splashes Werther with fountain water
    C. She berates Werther enthusiastically
    D. She tells the little girl a story

3. **What is the name of the woman whose deathbed Lotte attends?**
    A. Old M.
    B. Frau M.
    C. Lady S.
    D. Friedericke

4. **What secret does Frau M. reveal before dying?**
    A. That she has a horde of gold hidden in her mattress
    B. That she has never believed in the Bible
    C. That she has never been in love with her husband
    D. That she has taken money from her husband in order to meet weekly expenses

5. **Lotte plays the:**
    A. Lute
    B. Clavichord
    C. Fortepiano
    D. Harpsichord

6. **Werther is a:**
    A. Poor man
    B. Low–ranking noble
    C. Aristocrat
    D. Member of the bourgeoisie

7. **As a memento of Lotte, Werther:**
    A. Cuts her silhouette
    B. Takes one of her yellow ribbons
    C. Writes a sonnet on their first meeting
    D. Sketches her

8. **Which of the following does not describe Albert?**
    A. Cheerful
    B. Sensible
    C. Moody
    D. Hard–working

9. **Albert lends Werther:**
    A. His hunting pistols
    B. His copy of Homer
    C. A white scarf once worn by Lotte
    D. His copy of Ossian

10. **Werther and Albert debate:**
    A. The meaning of the story of Abraham and Isaac in the Bible
    B. The value of Klopstock's odes
    C. The merits of their respective educations
    D. The reasonableness of suicide

11. **Werther says that suicide is to mental suffering as:**
    A. A physician's treatment is to physical suffering
    B. Klopstock is to emotional suffering
    C. Death is to physical suffering
    D. Homicide is to immoral suffering

12. **When Albert arrives, Werther is:**
    A. Happy to spend time with him
    B. Determined to challange his claim to Lotte
    C. Accepting of his claim to Lotte
    D. Cast into turmoil

13. **Who advises Werther to apply for a position at Court?**
    A. Albert
    B. Wilhelm
    C. Werther's mother
    D. Lotte

14. **Why does Werther apply for a position at Court?**
    A. Because he cannot stand to be near Albert and Lotte
    B. Because his ambition is to be a high–ranking civil servant
    C. Because he feels that he needs to supply his own income before Lotte
    will consent to marry him
    D. Because he longs to be near Wilhelm again

15. **What does Albert give Werther for his birthday?**
    A. Ernesti's edition of Ossian
    B. Nothing
    C. Wettstein's edition of Homer
    D. One of Lotte's pink ribbons

16. **What does Lotte give Werther for his birthday?**
    A. A platonic kiss
    B. One of her pink ribbons
    C. The poems of Ossian
    D. Ernesti's edition of Homer

17. **Before leaving for his Court position, Werther:**
    A. Recites Lotte's siblings' favorite fairy tales by the fireside
    B. Contemplates suicide
    C. Tells Albert and Lotte the reason for his sudden departure
    D. Spends an evening discussing Lotte's deceased mother and the
    hereafter with Lotte and Albert

18. **Between Book One and Book Two how much time passes without a
    letter?**
    A. Ten days
    B. Two years
    C. Six months
    D. A month and ten days

19. **Which of the following does not describe the envoy?**
    A. Logical
    B. Emotive
    C. Envious
    D. Meticulous

20. **Who is Count C.?**
    A. A coldly rational man
    B. Fraulein von B.'s father
    C. A noble whom Werther befriends
    D. An amateur philologist

21. **While working in his official position, Werther is:**
    A. Often quite content
    B. Constantly suicidal
    C. Frustrated by class distinctions
    D. In love with Fraulein von B.

22. **Who disapproves of Werther's friendship with Fraulein von B.?**
    A. Wilhelm
    B. Her snobbish aunt
    C. Lotte
    D. Count C.

23. **As far as we know, how often does Werther write to Lotte while working in his official capacity?**
    A. Countless times
    B. Once
    C. Twice
    D. Never

24. **While he is working for the Court, what reminds Werther of his time with Lotte?**
    A. A ball he attends with Fraulein von B.
    B. A beautiful sunny day
    C. The atmosphere of a poor country inn
    D. The friendship he has with Count C.

25. The envoy:

A. Resigns after being snubbed at a party
B. Appreciates Werther's hard work
C. Is a good friend of Count C.'s
D. Disapproves of Werther's methods

Quiz 2 Answer Key

1. **(C)** He lifts her up and fervently kisses her
2. **(A)** She has the little girl wash her face in the spring water
3. **(B)** Frau M.
4. **(D)** That she has taken money from her husband in order to meet weekly expenses
5. **(B)** Clavichord
6. **(D)** Member of the bourgeoisie
7. **(A)** Cuts her silhouette
8. **(C)** Moody
9. **(A)** His hunting pistols
10. **(D)** The reasonableness of suicide
11. **(C)** Death is to physical suffering
12. **(D)** Cast into turmoil
13. **(B)** Wilhelm
14. **(A)** Because he cannot stand to be near Albert and Lotte
15. **(D)** One of Lotte's pink ribbons
16. **(D)** Ernesti's edition of Homer
17. **(D)** Spends an evening discussing Lotte's deceased mother and the hereafter with Lotte and Albert
18. **(D)** A month and ten days
19. **(B)** Emotive
20. **(C)** A noble whom Werther befriends
21. **(C)** Frustrated by class distinctions
22. **(B)** Her snobbish aunt
23. **(B)** Once
24. **(C)** The atmosphere of a poor country inn
25. **(D)** Disapproves of Werther's methods

Quiz 3

1. **What is the Minister's opinion of Werther?**
   A. He disapproves of Werther's nature
   B. He pays Werther no heed
   C. He finds Werther to be an arrogant bore
   D. He appreciates Werther's sensitivity

2. **When do Lotte and Albert tell Werther of their marriage?**
   A. After they have been married
   B. Just after Werther's mother has died
   C. A fortnight before the wedding
   D. They never tell him

3. **What does "en passant" mean?**
   A. "enough"
   B. "to take"
   C. "in passing"
   D. "impossible"

4. **Why is Werther at Count C.'s house on the night of an aristocratic gathering?**
   A. Because the Count and he live on the same property
   B. He heard of the party and decided to crash it
   C. The Count invited him to dinner
   D. To pay the Count a friendly visit

5. **Who asks Werther to leave the Count's party?**
   A. Fraulein von B.
   B. No one does; Werther feels the chill and simply leaves
   C. Lady S.
   D. Count C.

6. **What do people say about Werther after he is snubbed at the Count's party?**
   A. That Werther should resign from his post
   B. That he was uppity and had it coming
   C. That he was an innocent victim of misunderstanding
   D. That the Count should be ashamed

7. **After resigning from his Court position, with whom does Werther travel?**
   A. Prince ---
   B. Fraulein von B.
   C. Wilhelm
   D. Count C.

8. **Where does Werther go soon after resigning from his position?**
   A. His native town
   B. Wahlheim
   C. Count C.'s residence
   D. Italy

9. **When he is speaking of his native town, we learn that Werther:**
   A. Resents his mother for moving away from it
   B. Finds it boring and provincial
   C. Actually dislikes Homer
   D. Wants to stay there the rest of his life

10. **Which of these descriptions does Werther apply to the Prince?**
    A. Precise
    B. Emotional
    C. Turbulent
    D. Pseudo–scientific

11. **After leaving the Prince's estates, Werther:**
    A. Returns to his official position
    B. Travels for weeks on his own
    C. Goes to Wahlheim to be near Lotte
    D. Goes to his native village

12. **Upon returning to Wahlheim, Werther learns that:**
    A. Philip has died
    B. Lotte's father has died
    C. Hans has died
    D. Frau M. has died

13. **What happens when the country lad finally discloses his love to the widow?**
    A. She runs away from him
    B. She rebuffs him
    C. She marries him
    D. She promises him nothing

14. **What is Werther's customary garb?**
    A. Black from head to toe
    B. A white waist coat with tan breeches
    C. A blue frock coat and a yellow waist coat
    D. An oversized yellow coat and a French–style hat

15. **What happens with Lotte, Werther, and her little bird?**
    A. Werther frees her bird from its cage
    B. She gives the bird to Werther to take care of
    C. She sends the bird to Werther with messages
    D. She has the bird kiss her and then Werther

16. **The new minister's wife:**
    A. Has the walnut trees cut down
    B. Is meek and docile
    C. Is a proponent of Lavater
    D. Scandalously asks for a divorce

17. **In Book Two, who is Werther's favorite poet?**
    A. Ossian
    B. Schiller
    C. David
    D. Homer

18. **Who is Ossian's father?**
    A. Boromir
    B. Odin
    C. Ryno
    D. Fingal

19. Identify one of Werther's excesses in Book Two.
    A. He spends long evenings in front of his canvas, painting desperately
    B. He eats gluttonously
    C. He gambles all of his money away
    D. He drinks whole bottles of wine when he means to have just one glass

20. Which gospel reference does Werther NOT reference?
    A. Jesus exhortating his followers to emulate little children
    B. Jesus saying on the cross, "My God! Why hast thou forsaken me?"
    C. Jesus transforming of water into wine
    D. Jesus meeting with the woman at the well

21. Who is Heinrich?
    A. A madman in a green coat
    B. Lotte's third eldest brother
    C. The editor
    D. One of Werther's coworkers

22. What is a nosegay?
    A. A bouquet
    B. A vial of perfume
    C. A small citrus tree
    D. A hospitality gift

23. What part of his life does the madman look back upon contentedly?
    A. He is always content
    B. His childhood
    C. His time in the asylum
    D. His time with his beloved

24. Who reveals the full truth of Heinrich's history with Lotte?
    A. Albert
    B. Lotte's father
    C. Wilhelm
    D. Lotte

25. When tension is rife between her Werther, Lotte often:

A. Plays the clavichord

B. Reads to him from her translation of Ossian

C. Calls out to Albert

D. Excuses herself for a walk in the countryside

Quiz 3 Answer Key

1. **(D)** He appreciates Werther's sensitivity
2. **(A)** After they have been married
3. **(C)** "in passing"
4. **(C)** The Count invited him to dinner
5. **(D)** Count C.
6. **(B)** That he was uppity and had it coming
7. **(A)** Prince ---
8. **(A)** His native town
9. **(A)** Resents his mother for moving away from it
10. **(D)** Pseudo–scientific
11. **(C)** Goes to Wahlheim to be near Lotte
12. **(C)** Hans has died
13. **(B)** She rebuffs him
14. **(C)** A blue frock coat and a yellow waist coat
15. **(D)** She has the bird kiss her and then Werther
16. **(A)** Has the walnut trees cut down
17. **(A)** Ossian
18. **(D)** Fingal
19. **(D)** He drinks whole bottles of wine when he means to have just one glass
20. **(C)** Jesus transforming of water into wine
21. **(A)** A madman in a green coat
22. **(A)** A bouquet
23. **(C)** His time in the asylum
24. **(A)** Albert
25. **(A)** Plays the clavichord

Quiz 4

1. **Who is the editor most unlike in disposition?**
   A. Albert
   B. Goethe
   C. Wilhelm
   D. Werther

2. **How does the editor say he has gathered his information?**
   A. Through interviews
   B. Through primary documents
   C. Through intuition
   D. He doesn't say

3. **Werther feels that Albert:**
   A. Is a true initiate of Sturm und Drang
   B. Is irresponsible
   C. Does not pay enough attention to Lotte
   D. Is suicidal

4. **Who tells Werther of the murder of the widow's replacement for the country lad?**
   A. Albert
   B. Wilhelm
   C. The country lad
   D. Lotte's eldest brother

5. **Why does the country lad kill his replacement?**
   A. Because if he cannot have the widow, no one can
   B. Because he thinks that they will hire him back for his old job
   C. It was an accident; he didn't mean to
   D. Because he is insane

6. **To whom does Werther appeal for mercy in the country lad's case?**
   A. God
   B. The bailiff
   C. The minister
   D. Count C.

7. **Who does Werther NOT identify with?**
    A. Albert
    B. Salgar
    C. The country lad
    D. Heinrich

8. **Werther decides to commit suicide:**
    A. On his birthday
    B. On Lotte and Albert's anniversary
    C. In the heat of irrational passion
    D. With deliberate and cool premeditation

9. **What advice does Wilhelm give Werther?**
    A. To ask Lotte to divorce Albert
    B. To rebuke Count C. for his ill treatment at the dance
    C. To return to his birthplace before killing himself
    D. To leave Wahlheim and forget about Lotte

10. **Lotte tells Werther:**
    A. That she loves him more than Albert
    B. That she is going to name her first child after him
    C. That she thinks her unattainability is a great part of her attraction to him
    D. That his is the ideal character

11. **Near the end of his life, Lotte asks Werther:**
    A. Not to visit her before Christmas Eve
    B. To challange Albert for her hand
    C. To act as a father to her siblings
    D. To move away from Wahlheim

12. **When visiting Lotte for the last time, Werther:**
    A. Disobeys her wish that he not see her until Christmas Eve
    B. Brings Lotte his annotated copy of Ossian as a farewell present
    C. Shows uncharacteristic instability
    D. Tries to time his visit so that Albert would be there as well

13. **When Werther visits Lotte for the last time, Albert is:**
    A. In the room with them
    B. Asleep in his bedroom
    C. Hunting with friends
    D. Away on business

14. **What is Lotte's reaction upon hearing that Werther has come for his final visit?**
    A. She tries to send for some friends so as not to be alone with him
    B. She promises to divorce Albert and elope with him
    C. She sends away her friends so as to be alone with him
    D. She shuts herself in her room and refuses to see him

15. **Who translated the passages from Ossian that Werther reads aloud?**
    A. Werther
    B. Schelling
    C. Goldsmith
    D. Klopstock

16. **Which word does NOT describe Lotte and Werther's reaction to the reading of Ossian?**
    A. Identification
    B. Sorrowful
    C. Distraught
    D. Placid

17. **After reading Ossian, Werther:**
    A. Immediately shoots himself
    B. Can't stop himself from kissing Lotte
    C. Finds himself purged of his infatuation with Lotte
    D. Says that he prefers Homer

18. **How do we know that Werther climbed a steep bluff on the night of his suicide?**
    A. His hat was found at the bluff later
    B. His footprints were visible
    C. He told Lotte that he had done so
    D. He wrote about climbing the bluff in his suicide note

19. **Which of the following does Werther NOT say after kissing Lotte?**
    A. That the kiss did not mean anything
    B. That he wishes she would forgive him
    C. That he feels her kisses still
    D. That she is eternally his

20. **Who does Werther say he will meet in the hereafter?**
    A. Ossian
    B. Lotte's mother
    C. God
    D. His mother

21. **Who doesn't play a part in securing for Werther the fatal weapons on the night of his suicide?**
    A. Albert
    B. The bailiff
    C. Werther's servant
    D. Lotte

22. **Which of the following is NOT one of Wether's last requests?**
    A. That he be buried with Lotte's ribbon
    B. That no one look through his pockets
    C. That he be buried in the clothes he is wearing
    D. That his mother be notified of his death

23. **Who finds Werther's dying body?**
    A. Albert
    B. A neighbor who heard the shot
    C. His servant
    D. Lotte

24. **What book is open on Werther's writing desk when his dying body is found?**
    A. Ossian's Poems
    B. Homer's Odyssey
    C. Klopstock's Odes
    D. Lessing's Emilia Galotti

25. **Which of the following is NOT true of Werther's burial service?**
     A. Lotte and Albert do not attend
     B. No clergymen attend the burial
     C. Workmen carry his coffin
     D. Werther's mother attends the ceremony

Quiz 4 Answer Key

1. (**D**) Werther
2. (**A**) Through interviews
3. (**C**) Does not pay enough attention to Lotte
4. (**D**) Lotte's eldest brother
5. (**A**) Because if he cannot have the widow, no one can
6. (**B**) The bailiff
7. (**A**) Albert
8. (**D**) With deliberate and cool premeditation
9. (**D**) To leave Wahlheim and forget about Lotte
10. (**C**) That she thinks her unattainability is a great part of her attraction to him
11. (**A**) Not to visit her before Christmas Eve
12. (**A**) Disobeys her wish that he not see her until Christmas Eve
13. (**D**) Away on business
14. (**A**) She tries to send for some friends so as not to be alone with him
15. (**A**) Werther
16. (**D**) Placid
17. (**B**) Can't stop himself from kissing Lotte
18. (**A**) His hat was found at the bluff later
19. (**A**) That the kiss did not mean anything
20. (**B**) Lotte' s mother
21. (**B**) The bailiff
22. (**D**) That his mother be notified of his death
23. (**C**) His servant
24. (**D**) Lessing's Emilia Galotti
25. (**D**) Werther's mother attends the ceremony

ClassicNotes

GrAdeSaver™

Getting you the grade since 1999™

Other ClassicNotes from GradeSaver™

1984
Absalom, Absalom
Adam Bede
The Adventures of Augie
  March
The Adventures of
  Huckleberry Finn
The Adventures of Tom
  Sawyer
The Aeneid
Agamemnon
The Age of Innocence
Alice in Wonderland
All My Sons
All Quiet on the Western
  Front
All the King's Men
All the Pretty Horses
The Ambassadors
American Beauty
Angela's Ashes
Animal Farm
Anna Karenina
Antigone
Antony and Cleopatra
Aristotle's Ethics
Aristotle's Poetics
Aristotle's Politics
As I Lay Dying
As You Like It
The Awakening
Babbitt
The Bacchae
Bartleby the Scrivener
The Bean Trees
The Bell Jar

Beloved
Benito Cereno
Beowulf
Billy Budd
Black Boy
Bleak House
Bluest Eye
Brave New World
Breakfast at Tiffany's
Call of the Wild
Candide
The Canterbury Tales
Cat's Cradle
Catch-22
The Catcher in the Rye
The Caucasian Chalk
  Circle
The Cherry Orchard
The Chosen
A Christmas Carol
Chronicle of a Death
  Foretold
Civil Disobedience
Civilization and Its
  Discontents
A Clockwork Orange
The Color of Water
The Color Purple
Comedy of Errors
Communist Manifesto
A Confederacy of
  Dunces
Connecticut Yankee in
  King Arthur's Court
Coriolanus

The Count of Monte
  Cristo
Crime and Punishment
The Crucible
Cry, the Beloved
  Country
The Crying of Lot 49
Cymbeline
Daisy Miller
Death in Venice
Death of a Salesman
The Death of Ivan Ilych
Democracy in America
Devil in a Blue Dress
The Diary of Anne Frank
Disgrace
Divine Comedy-I:
  Inferno
A Doll's House
Don Quixote Book I
Don Quixote Book II
Dr. Faustus
Dr. Jekyll and Mr. Hyde
Dracula
Dubliners
East of Eden
Emma
Ender's Game
Endgame
Ethan Frome
The Eumenides
Everything is Illuminated
Fahrenheit 451
The Fall of the House of
  Usher
Farewell to Arms

For our full list of over 250 Study Guides, Quizzes,
Sample College Application Essays, Literature Essays and E-texts, visit:

www.gradesaver.com

ClassicNotes

GrAdeSaver™

Getting you the grade since 1999™

Other ClassicNotes from GradeSaver™

The Federalist Papers
For Whom the Bell Tolls
The Fountainhead
Frankenstein
Franny and Zooey
Glass Menagerie
The God of Small Things
The Grapes of Wrath
Great Expectations
The Great Gatsby
Hamlet
The Handmaid's Tale
Hard Times
Heart of Darkness
Hedda Gabler
Henry IV (Pirandello)
Henry IV Part 1
Henry IV Part 2
Henry V
The Hobbit
Homo Faber
House of Mirth
House of the Seven
    Gables
The House of the Spirits
House on Mango Street
Howards End
A Hunger Artist
I Know Why the Caged
    Bird Sings
An Ideal Husband
Iliad
The Importance of Being
    Earnest
In Our Time
Inherit the Wind

Invisible Man
The Island of Dr. Moreau
Jane Eyre
Jazz
The Joy Luck Club
Julius Caesar
Jungle of Cities
Kidnapped
King Lear
Last of the Mohicans
Leviathan
Libation Bearers
The Lion, the Witch and
    the Wardrobe
Lolita
Long Day's Journey Into
    Night
Lord Jim
Lord of the Flies
The Lord of the Rings:
    The Fellowship of the
    Ring
The Lord of the Rings:
    The Return of the
    King
The Lord of the Rings:
    The Two Towers
A Lost Lady
The Love Song of J.
    Alfred Prufrock
Lucy
Macbeth
Madame Bovary
Manhattan Transfer
Mansfield Park
MAUS

The Mayor of
    Casterbridge
Measure for Measure
Medea
Merchant of Venice
Metamorphoses
The Metamorphosis
Middlemarch
Midsummer Night's
    Dream
Moby Dick
Moll Flanders
Mother Courage and Her
    Children
Mrs. Dalloway
Much Ado About
    Nothing
My Antonia
Native Son
Night
No Exit
Notes from Underground
O Pioneers
The Odyssey
Oedipus Rex / Oedipus
    the King
Of Mice and Men
The Old Man and the Sea
On Liberty
One Day in the Life of
    Ivan Denisovich
One Flew Over the
    Cuckoo's Nest
One Hundred Years of
    Solitude
Oroonoko

For our full list of over 250 Study Guides, Quizzes,
Sample College Application Essays, Literature Essays and E-texts, visit:

www.gradesaver.com

ClassicNotes

GrAdeSaver™

Getting you the grade since 1999™

Other ClassicNotes from GradeSaver™

Othello
Our Town
Pale Fire
Paradise Lost
A Passage to India
The Pearl
The Picture of Dorian
   Gray
Poems of W.B. Yeats:
   The Rose
Portrait of the Artist as a
   Young Man
Pride and Prejudice
Prometheus Bound
Pudd'nhead Wilson
Pygmalion
Rabbit, Run
A Raisin in the Sun
The Real Life of
   Sebastian Knight
Red Badge of Courage
The Republic
Richard II
Richard III
The Rime of the Ancient
   Mariner
Robinson Crusoe
Roll of Thunder, Hear
   My Cry
Romeo and Juliet
A Room of One's Own
A Room With a View
Rosencrantz and
   Guildenstern Are
   Dead
Salome

The Scarlet Letter
Secret Sharer
Sense and Sensibility
A Separate Peace
Shakespeare's Sonnets
Siddhartha
Silas Marner
Sir Gawain and the
   Green Knight
Sister Carrie
Six Characters in Search
   of an Author
Slaughterhouse Five
Snow Falling on Cedars
The Social Contract
Something Wicked This
   Way Comes
Song of Roland
Sons and Lovers
The Sorrows of Young
   Werther
The Sound and the Fury
Spring Awakening
The Stranger
A Streetcar Named
   Desire
The Sun Also Rises
Tale of Two Cities
The Taming of the Shrew
The Tempest
Tender is the Night
Tess of the D'Urbervilles
Their Eyes Were
   Watching God
Things Fall Apart
The Threepenny Opera

The Time Machine
Titus Andronicus
To Build a Fire
To Kill a Mockingbird
To the Lighthouse
Treasure Island
Troilus and Cressida
Turn of the Screw
Twelfth Night
Ulysses
Uncle Tom's Cabin
Utopia
A Very Old Man With
   Enormous Wings
The Visit
Volpone
Waiting for Godot
Waiting for Lefty
Walden
Washington Square
Where the Red Fern
   Grows
White Fang
White Noise
White Teeth
Who's Afraid of Virginia
   Woolf
Winesburg, Ohio
The Winter's Tale
Woyzeck
Wuthering Heights
The Yellow Wallpaper
Yonnondio: From the
   Thirties

For our full list of over 250 Study Guides, Quizzes,
Sample College Application Essays, Literature Essays and E-texts, visit:

www.gradesaver.com